You Can Be Rich by Thursday

or

The Secrets Of Making A Fortune In Multi-Level Marketing

By Tom Pinnock

Pinnock, Tom
You Can Be Rich By Thursday: The Secrets Of Making a Fortune In Multi-Level Marketing

ISBN # 1-882467-14-0

Library Of Congress Catalog Card # 96-61714

Cover Design: Davison and Associates

Also available on audio cassette
To order Wildstone books and cassettes call toll free:
(800) 296-1918

Wildstone Media
401 Bussen Underground Rd.
St. Louis, MO 63129
(314) 487-0402

Introduction

The title of the book is ludicrous of course. It was meant to be. But the subtitle is on target. I know, because Tom Pinnock has been through the entire song and dance from being poor and desperate to finding a niche and with it some hope, and then working that hope into a dream that became his reality.

This is Tom's story, but he has convinced me that it could be anyone's. Instant wealth happens in fairy tales, the entertainment business and crime. However, I agreed to edit this book because Tom represents the modern American dream. He is an individual who worked his way up to the pinnacle of his profession and became rich in the process.

Tom demonstrates that in multi-level marketing anyone who's trainable, has determination and is willing to exert himself can become a millionaire. There is nothing instant about the process, but it doesn't have to take a lifetime, not even a dog's lifetime.

This book will show you how it can be accomplished. There is no magic involved, and even with occasional speed bumps, the path is clear. It's just a matter of finding the path and taking the first step.

Dick Richmond

Acknowledgments

This is a book I have been burning to write for several years as a tool to help people in multi-level marketing. However, the project probably would have never gotten off the ground if Dick Richmond had not been there to guide me through the entire process from outline to completion, editing and encouraging me every step of the way. Then, after the manuscript was completed, Dick enlisted Dr. Jack G. Shaheen, professor emeritus of mass communications at Southern Illinois University, to lend his critical eye to the project. I owe him thanks for his many helpful suggestions.

Chapter 1

A Bump In The Night

"The only problem I had with being poor was that I never had any money."   — Tom Pinnock

I n the late 1980s, my family and I lived in a small starter home that backed up to a swamp in Central Florida. Karen, my beautiful bride, used to say that the cockroaches in our house were as big as the alligators in the backyard. That's a bit of an exaggeration, though I must confess that a couple of mean roaches once chased me out of the garage.

Like so many families, we struggled to make ends meet. Our three children, Lindsay, 6, Tommy, 3, and Ashley, 1, filled our home with love. But we had a heck of a time filling our cars with gas and our cabinets with groceries. Having a savings account then was just a concept. I used to tell folks, "that we were so poor we couldn't afford a dog. If we heard a noise outside, we'd just sit up in bed and bark ourselves." People always laughed, but deep down inside it made me sad. Too close to the truth, I guess.

It wasn't that we weren't working hard to get ahead. It's just that we weren't getting much monetary value for the hours that we invested in our jobs. I was a reporter for the Orlando Sentinel and Karen was a nurse caring for outpatients in their homes.

At the time, Lindsay was in elementary school, and Tommy and Ashley spent their days at child care. This was especially tough because Ashley was still a baby. Karen and I dreaded dropping the kids off at daycare in the morning. They cried hard when we did, and it made us feel so guilty.

"Don't leave me, don't leave me, Daddy," Tommy would plead each day. "I want to stay with you."

"It's OK, little buddy," I remember telling him one morning as I fought back tears. "Next weekend, I'm going to take you to Disney World."

Immediately, a big smile spread across his freckled face. As he wiped away the tears from his cheeks, he asked, "Will I get to see Goofy? I like Goofy."

"You bet, and Mickey Mouse, too," I added.

From that moment on, Tommy counted the days until our little vacation. And while the kids waited impatiently, Karen and I saved every dime we could get our hands on. Disney World was the one place the children wanted to go to more than any other. They couldn't understand why we had never taken them there before, considering that we lived less than an hour away. It's not easy to tell your children that you can't afford to do some of the things they want and deserve.

Anticipating this little adventure, we had cut back in every area we could. For weeks, we hadn't gone to the movies or out to eat. Haircuts at a barber became a thing of the past. We even began packing our lunches for work. To top it off, we had a garage sale so that by the time we were scheduled to go, we had managed to save nearly $500, which was more than enough for a nice weekend at the Magic Kingdom.

The night before our journey down Interstate 4 to Disney World, I had to work very late in order to finish a story. It was one of those investigative reports that involved a lot of research and an enormous amount of footwork. It was something that I had been involved with for almost three weeks and it was to be the lead on the front page for that Sunday's paper. So by the time I handed it in, I was drained, not only physically but intellectually and emotionally as well.

As I drove home, it was well after midnight and there was no traffic to speak of. Without knowing why, the broken white lines in the middle of the road suddenly seemed to capture my attention. In spite of my fatigue, a warmth had come over me. But all I can remember is that one moment I was thinking about how much fun the kids were going to have at Disney World, and the next I had crashed into the side of a bridge. Just for an instant, my eyes must have closed.

Fortunately, I hadn't been traveling fast, so I was shocked but unhurt. The van wasn't as fortunate. The right front tire was flat and the wheel caved in. A strut had been broken and a shock bent. In addition, the right front fender was twisted and loose.

There was nothing to do but call a wrecker. To make matters worse, I hadn't been able to afford collision insurance, which meant that I had to pay for the damages out of my own pocket.

"How much you figure this is going to cost me?" I nervously asked the tow-truck driver as he backed my heap into a parking space in front of his garage.

"Hard to tell," he said, shaking his head in the way that only a garage man can. "Probably be a good six or seven hundred dollars, though."

"That much?" I asked.

"Afraid so. Might be cheaper if I can find some used parts. Got insurance, don't you?"

"No," I said, "but I've saved some money, and I need it fixed right away. I got to have the van for work."

"Won't take me long to get her back on the road," he said. "Just as long as you got the money."

"Don't worry, you'll get paid," I answered, and as I turned and walked away, I thought to myself, "there goes our little vacation."

I was sick to my stomach as I trudged the two or three miles to the house. Karen would have picked me up if I had telephoned, but I didn't want to wake her. Besides, there was no need to share bad news in the middle of the night, especially when I was angry and frustrated.

Knowing that I had worked into the wee hours of the morning in order to meet my deadline, Karen let me sleep late. I didn't stir until Tommy jumped in bed with me.

"Wake up Daddy," he whispered in my ear. "It's time to go see Goofy."

At first, I had forgotten about smashing up the van the night before. Then, I remembered and all I wanted to do was slap myself. Lindsay stood in the doorway, her suitcase in hand. She, too, was ready for the weekend excursion. Behind her, I saw Karen holding Ashley in her arms. They were all dressed, packed and ready to roll. I got up slowly, gave them all a half-hearted kiss, and then asked to speak to Karen alone.

"Honey, I've got some bad news," I said, trying not to look into her eyes. "I wrecked the van."

"You did what?" she asked.

"I fell asleep coming home last night and plowed into a concrete wall."

Bam, bam, bam. "It's time to go, Daddy," chimed the kids in unison as they impatiently knocked on the bedroom door.

"We'll be out in a minute," I said, harshly.

"Don't tell me this means we can't take the kids to Disney World," Karen said in disbelief. "They'll be heartbroken."

"I've got to fix the van, honey. What do you want me to do?"

"I want you to tell the kids," she said, her blue eyes filling with tears. "I can't do it. I won't do it."

With that, Karen went into the bathroom and shut the door. I could hear her crying as I walked out into the living room to face the children.

I set them down on the couch and broke the news as gently as I knew how. Tommy and Lindsay both looked at me in disbelief. Then, they began to cry as they ran off in search of their mother.

"This isn't fair, it isn't fair," I heard Lindsay plead as she pounded on the bathroom door. Tommy cried out, "No, Mommy, no, Mommy."

I walked out into the backyard to get away from the weeping, and there, as I placed my head against a tree, I shed tears of my own.

"I'm such a rotten father," I thought to myself. "I can't even take my family off for a weekend."

Chapter 2

Looking For Another Way

*"How can a poor man become rich, or has the American
dream become as rare as homemade apple pie?"*   —TP

F rom the day I had to tell Karen and the kids that I couldn't
take them to Disney World, I was determined to become a
better provider for my family. I swore that the moment
would come when my children would visit that land of enchant-
ment and see Goofy and all his friends in style. The problem was
figuring out how to do it.

Corporate America obviously wasn't the answer to riches. There
was a time, of course, when a person could strive with an organization in a mutual exchange of loyalty for 30 years or more, then
retire with dignity, earning a pension and a gold watch. But that
day had passed, bowing out with the corporate greed of the '80s
in which so many good companies were dismantled for the benefit
of the few.

In earlier decades, massive layoffs meant the man at the top
wasn't doing his job properly, but by the beginning of the '90s,
CEOs of the some of the largest companies in the United States
were being applauded by Wall Street for their slasher techniques.
Cutting tens of thousands of people from the ranks of their companies may have made investors happy, but in so doing they

introduced misery and uncertainty into the lives of countless numbers of families. What added insult to injury was that the slashers were enriching themselves in the process.

Downsizing was becoming the favorite catchword, a public relations term that was supposed to make the cancer that was raging through corporate ranks seem like something other than the disease that it was. In spite of the fact that news magazines were printing articles warning of the fear that was flowing into the ranks of the white collar worker, and the potential backlash, more and more companies joined in as Corporate America rushed to discard its conscience.

Being a newspaper man, I had a pretty good grasp on reality, and I knew that whining about change was not going to halt it. I was used to reading the news and absorbing what I read. I didn't equate a computer giant's cutting 60,000 jobs or communication company's severing more than 30,000 as just numbers. I had been on stories in which I saw families financially shattered as men and women were put out to pasture before their time and prior to their pensions kicking in. To me, these occurrences were worse than some natural disasters, because they had been caused by intelligent men, perhaps some of the best that America had to offer.

"Unnatural disasters," I thought. "That's what these men are creating."

Thousands of people were being laid off because of downsizing, mergers and plant closings.

"And that's only the beginning," my colleagues in the newsroom would say to one another as business news regularly made its way onto the front page. "Automation and computers will make a lot more jobs obsolete."

So with what was happening in the shifting job market, I considered going into business for myself. After all, it doesn't take a genius to figure out that you are never going to get ahead working for someone else. The problem was that starting my own business took money, a lot of money. More than that, I wasn't exactly certain where my talents lay. I had been a tank commander in the

Army, a firefighter and a newspaper man. So I had to investigate the possibilities. That, at least, I knew how to do.

I looked into hamburger franchises in which the start-up costs were well over $100,000. Then I sought out an outfit that wanted more than $30,000 for the privilege of changing someone's smelly oil. But that didn't stop me from my upward march to other things I couldn't afford. I also explored a popular restaurant chain that demanded in excess of a $1 million to put its name on an establishment that would be all mine and several banks. Considering that it was all I could do to get my junky van out of the shop and buy a used tire, my situation looked grim.

Not only were the startup costs too high for me to open a business, but so were the risks. Imagine having to borrow $50,000 to get your dream off the ground. Talk about going into debt. Of course, that was really a non-problem for me, because no one in their right mind was going to lend me money that had a lot of zeros in it.

Furthermore, regardless of how much cash or credit I sank into my enterprise, there were no guarantees for success. All I had to do was drive through the commercial area in my home town to see where new businesses had come and gone as rapidly as the changing of the seasons. They were monuments to broken dreams and ravaged bank accounts of entrepreneurs everywhere.

Also, I had no knowledge about running my own business. Oh sure, in the Army I had learned how to maneuver a tank company into battle, but that wasn't the same as keeping track of expenses, accounts receivable, employee compensation and social security taxes. Obviously, at gunpoint, I could probably take over a community, but in a battle for customers in that same community, I might be the one who'd have to surrender.

I mentioned being a firefighter. It's true. Two of the best years of my life were spent putting out flames for the Orlando Fire Department. Great training, but the department didn't teach me a thing about such burning business issues as product research and marketing. Due diligence, which is the painstaking exploration of a business' potential, wasn't even in my vocabulary then.

As a journalist, I could turn a phrase, but could I turn a profit.

On top of all this, there was the problem of time. As it was, I was already spending too much time away from my family working for other people. I didn't know much about business, but I did know that owners generally put in more hours working for themselves than they ever did laboring for someone else. Becoming a slave to a dream was one thing but toiling my life away in a business was another. I needed more time with Karen and the children, not less.

As I went through the process of winnowing out the things I didn't want to do to become rich, I entered a highly analytic stage of my life. I knew, for instance, that I was not going to borrow lots of money nor sign a long-term lease and rent lots of equipment. Carrying a large inventory or taking employees under my wing seemed like a bummer, too. Most of all, I was not going to put in long hours. There had to be a better way, and I was determined to keep winnowing until I found what it was.

Maybe I could become a big-time investor as was suggested to me by a man who became one of America's great success stories.

In the middle 1980s, I interviewed the late Sam Walton when he was in Kissimmee, Florida, opening one of his Wal-Mart stores. I invited him to lunch.

It was pretty exciting. One of the richest men in America was going to break bread with me and, perhaps, share some of his secrets of success. We met at the snack bar in his new store. Not exactly big time, but I couldn't complain, because he immediately gave me a lesson in how the rich get richer by having me pick up the tab.

As the gray-haired business giant pulled on his chocolate milk, I popped the million dollar question. "Mr. Walton," I asked, "what would a fellow like me need to do to make a lot of money like you?"

This man who was famous for not being open around the press carefully put down his milk and regarded me seriously for a long moment. "Why, son," he said, "you need to take every penny you have and buy as much Wal-Mart stock as you can."

"That's all?" I asked.

"That's it," he said.

He was absolutely correct. If I had taken his advice and invested thousands in Wal-Mart back then, I would have been one fat cat right now. Of course, I am one fat cat right now, but Sam Walton's not the reason. His advice to me was about as good as Marie Antoinette's when she was told that the multitudes had no bread and responded by saying, "Let 'em eat cake." That was my situation back then. I had no bread, and he was suggesting cake.

That, however, did not keep me from being temporarily excited about his piece of wisdom. I remember coming home after that interview and excitedly telling Karen that I had the secret to becoming filthy rich.

"Honey," I blurted out when I saw Karen, "Sam Walton told me how we can make a fortune. It's so simple."

"What do we have to do?" she asked.

"Buy Wal-Mart stock."

"That's great," she answered. "But don't you think we need to pay our overdue electric and phone bills first?"

"Right," I said, "Wal-Mart stock is out. Street of gold, too, I guess."

And I never bought one share of Wal-Mart stock, but a few years later, I found my street of gold via an avenue called network marketing. It was on that avenue that I came to learn about people who dare to dream big and then go on to change their lives forever. Network marketing is the path I followed and it made me rich.

Chapter 3

Window Of Opportunity

*"I would rather have one percent of the efforts of a hundred
people than a hundred percent of my own efforts."*
                                        — John Paul Getty

few weeks after the Disney disaster, Karen and I walked
out to my van in a parking lot at a mall near our home in
Longwood, Florida, and found a business opportunity card
stuck to the windshield. Ordinarily, I threw such things away
without even bothering to read them, but this time I didn't. As I
gathered the card in like a fish gobbling up a baited hook, Karen
couldn't suppress a smile.

"They took one look at your old van and figured you needed
an opportunity," she said, giggling in that cute little way she has.

"Don't be making fun of my van," I said, pretending to be
offended. "She's got a brand new used tire on the front."

"Right," she said. "I forgot."

"The change in her condition is pretty subtle," I conceded,
kicking the new used tire before helping Karen into the old rust
bucket.

After I got behind the wheel, I read the card out loud:

*"If you're not making $10,000 a month,
I'll show you how. Call 24 hours a day
for a message that could change your life..."*

"Can you imagine making $10,000 in one month?" I asked Karen as I stuck the card into my pocket. "Do you think this is for real?"

"I doubt it," she said. "But let's call and see what it's all about. Who knows, if I can make that kind of money, I might splurge and buy you a brand new tire."

"How about a red Mercedes convertible?"

"Nope, just a tire," she said.

"You're too good to me, darling."

Later that day, my curiosity getting the better of me, I called the number written on the card and listened to a message. Since I hadn't left the Sentinel yet, my attitude was pretty objective. A man's voice told of an incredible opportunity involving unique products, and the need for people who weren't afraid to work hard and dream big. The man sounded very excited, and the message ended with an invitation to come to an evening meeting at a nearby country club. I called the number again so Karen could listen, too. After the second call, I felt a spark of electricity surge through me, but mixed in with it was a dash of fear because I then knew the direction I would be taking.

Unfortunately, the meeting took place on a night that I had to work. Karen, however, was as curious as I was, so she got a sitter to watch the children so that she could go. I couldn't wait to get home from work that night to hear what she had learned.

"How was the meeting?" I asked when I walked in the door. "Are we going to start making $10,000 a month?"

Karen smiled, thought for a moment — probably about how it would feel to make that kind of money — and then began telling me about her night.

"It was very interesting," she said. "There were perhaps 50 people there. Among them was a very sharp woman who said she was making about $25,000 a month selling skin-care products for a company called Nu Skin."

"Twenty-five thousand dollars a month selling skin-care products?" I gasped. "You've got to be kidding?"

"That's what she said."

"What's Nu Skin?" I asked. "I've never heard of it."

"It's one of those — what did she call it? Multi-level marketing companies. Maybe she said network marketing. I don't remember for certain, but it was something like that."

"Like Amway," I said. "One of those pyramid deals."

"Yeah, I guess," Karen answered. "The woman said a lot of companies were involved in multi-level marketing now: MCI, U.S. Sprint, Rexall and Avon among them."

When she said U.S. Sprint, I cringed. A good friend of ours, Dale Fowler, had gotten involved with Network 2000 Marketing, which was a network-marketing operation for U.S. Sprint. On a number of occasions, he had tried to discuss what he was doing with me, and I refused to listen. Much to my amazement, he went on to make a fortune, and I sat wondering how he did it.

"What else did you learn?" I asked.

"This woman said some guy named Mark Yarnell was making a whole lot more money than she was."

"That's ridiculous," I said. "How could you make more than $25,000 a month selling skin-care products?"

Karen shrugged, then said, "I don't know, but when she was explaining it, the program made sense to me. She used a big white board and diagrammed how it is being done. It's because you get paid commissions for your sales plus the sales of people you bring into the business."

"What did the guy on the business card have to say about it?" I asked. "Was he making that kind of money, too?"

"I never saw him," Karen said. "It was kind of strange, too, because no one talked to me after the meeting was over, so I just left."

Although Karen left her name and number, no one followed up with us. Consequently, we didn't sign on with Nu Skin. I later learned about Mark Yarnell and how he had become a millionaire in the business. In fact, he became a legend in the network-marketing industry. I know now that he is not the kind of individual who would have let us get away without, at least, a follow-up telephone call.

Although I didn't attend the meeting, I was intrigued and decided to learn all I could about multi-level marking (MLM) companies, and maybe, just maybe, find one that suited me. I was like an old hound dog who had the scent of something good, I just didn't know what it was yet. The one thought that kept going through my mind was that if this worked for some people, it might function for me, too.

In the months that followed, I learned that multi-level marketing had been around for decades, getting its biggest boost when Amway moved into the field. Amway was founded in 1959 by Rich DeVos and Jay Van Andel, who have become two of the richest men in America, according to Forbes magazine. Recently, it was reported that Amway's sales were in the neighborhood of $5 billion annually, a billion in Japan alone. That's a neighborhood without a swamp.

But it wasn't just the founders of Amway who made a lot of money. One of the company's top distributors, Dexter Yager, who used to be a brewery salesman making less than $100 a week, is estimated by industry experts to be earning more than $10 million a year.

Another company, Shaklee, was founded in 1956 by Dr. Forrest C. Shaklee. It is a respected nutritional-foods company, and top performers are reported to be earning more than $500,000 annually.

Such numbers made me weak, dazzling my perceptions of what reality was for others, people who had achieved a fortune through their own efforts. At the time that I began my investigation into the MLMs, I thought I would be delighted to be making $30,000 a year, working out of my home and being my own boss. Obviously, my basis in fact was limited by my experience. I had met rich people, but I really couldn't think of myself as being rich. Don't misunderstand. I wanted wealth, but I had yet to leap over the wall that prevented me from seeing how I could work my way into Ali Baba's cave. Part of the reason, of course, was that I was handicapped by skepticism ingrained in me as a reporter.

Still, I couldn't argue the fact that network marketing was a proven means of distributing goods, and that millions of people across the world were doing it successfully. I had to make myself visualize me in that successful crowd.

Whereas my involvement in newspaper business handicapped me in one way, it benefited me in many others, not the least of which was the fact that I knew how to dig and keep from making assumptions until I had all the facts in hand.

I don't have to remind you that when Karen first explained to me what she had learned at the Nu Skin meeting, I blurted out what I then knew about multi-level marketing. I said, "Pyramid deal." That was before I began doing my research.

I was learning that some business-watchers were referring to MLM as the silent revolution, in which a bunch of regular people were banding together and moving products through their own established networks and, therefore, sharing in the available wealth. Instead of going to the shopping centers and buying from strangers, they were buying from one another, and thus were supporting one another. It was the power of word-of-mouth advertising versus mass-media advertising.

In other words, instead of a company paying a sports star $2 million to go on television and talk about how much he liked a product, an MLM was using independent contractors to attract customers. In that way, the MLM was able to market its products less expensively and then was able to reward its distributors by dividing the $2 million among them.

In fact, I was learning that the MLM companies were paying distributors not only for their personal sales, but also the sales of their personal network reaching down several levels.

It is important to clarify this, so I'm going to put it another way. What I discovered was that the MLMs were not only paying their direct sellers commissions on their personal sales, but encouraging these direct sellers to sponsor others. The individuals who were brought into the network by the sponsor then became part of that sponsor's group. The sponsor added to his earnings by what his group sold. Of course, the bigger the group, the more money the sponsor made.

But commissions often went beyond personal individual sponsorship. An individual brought into the group could then become a sponsor, too. And the new sponsor's candidate would become part of the original sponsor's group as well. And this would repeat itself sometimes as deep as five and six levels down, into a complex multi-level network, all earning and all passing the commissions upward.

Obviously, the reason the networkers could be rewarded for their efforts in such an advantageous system was because the company didn't have to pay all the middlemen — wholesalers, jobbers, retailers, and advertisers. There was only one middleman. As a result, the compensation was much higher.

Another advantage for the MLM entrepreneur was that start-up costs were low, usually the price of a distributor kit, which was generally less than $50. That means the average person could get into the system with little risk.

Not only that, but because it was to the advantage of the individuals in the direct upline to have a new distributor become successful, experienced distributors were there to advise, assist and train newcomers at no cost.

In addition, there was the relief in regard to some other issues so often troubling to someone starting a business. As examples, the company took care of shipping products, taking orders, research and development, legal aspects, accounting and all those things that most of us know nothing about.

The more I learned about network marketing, the more I liked it. The big question was finding the right company for me.

Chapter 4

Picking The Right Company For You

"Even if you're on the right track, you're going to get run over by a train unless you get moving."   — Will Rogers

The first thing I did in my search for an MLM company was to eliminate all the "get rich schemes." They're easy enough to spot inasmuch as they all seem to be offering an opportunity to be a millionaire by the end of the month, and you can pick the month. Most of the time with these companies, actual work does not seem to be part of the game plan. If you can breathe and you've got a few thousand bucks, you're in. Sometimes it doesn't even matter if you can breathe.

According to these carpetbaggers, success happens magically. All you have to do is sign up, invest a tidy sum, and get a bunch of other suckers to do the same. Forget about product. The appeal of such operations are greed and laziness, and they flourish because some people still think they can get something for nothing.

Even before I began my investigations, I had read enough for me to stay clear of anyone who suggested that money could be made without moving products or providing a service. I was dealing with the future of my family, and wasn't about to taint it with some sleight-of-hand contrivance. Magic indeed.

Unfortunately, the wannabe Merlins have left many people believing that all MLMs are scams, illegal pyramids, or elaborate forms of a chain letter. It stands to reason that the best and the worst people are attracted to an opportunity that offers high rewards and low start-up cost. But the key word to any legitimate program is work. You have to work to make it function.

It didn't take long to figure out that reputable MLM companies offered quality products at a fair price. Also, they didn't require new distributors to purchase thousands of dollars worth of merchandise that might take several years if not a lifetime or three to market. This is a despicable practice known as front-end loading.

A front-end loading networker once sold a boatload of water filters to one of my best friends. He had water filters in his garage, attic and basement. He might even have had a couple in his doghouse. Each year, for my birthday, he sent me a water filter. Though he had plenty of clean drinking water, the experience left him bitter. As a result, it was years before he would consider another MLM company.

Another thing that alerted my early warning systems was MLM companies offering big bucks just for signing people into their program. To make money in an MLM, products or services must be sold, which means getting customers. In many places, it is illegal to pay big bonuses just for recruiting.

Then, while sorting through MLMs, I discovered that many have a good buy-back policy, which became one of my measuring sticks in judging a company. That simply means that a company will repurchase products and sales aids that are in resalable condition from distributors who want to quit the program. In addition, the top MLMs also offer customers a money-back guarantee on their products.

Another concern was training. Since I had no MLM experience, it was essential for me to find a company that had on-the-job training as part of company policy. I had an aptitude for hosing down fires and flushing out snipers because I was taught how to do those things. It was obvious to me that I needed guidance in order to build an effective distribution system.

With that in mind, I was able to eliminate a lot of companies just by looking at their marketing materials. If their opportunity videos and product brochures were shabby, it stood to reason that the company was not first class.

For example, one night, Karen and I put in an opportunity video that was so bad it almost put an end to my MLM career before it started. It showed a bunch of people with commission checks plastered to their forehead jumping up and down and screaming. Karen was horrified, and the kids ran out of the room.

"What's the rating on that movie?" Lindsay called over her shoulder as she walked away.

"If this is what multi-level marketing is all about, I think I'd rather be poor," Karen mumbled as she pushed the eject button.

The video, which was shot at a national conference, was awful, but I learned something from it. Before I'd get too involved with an MLM, I would make a point of attending one of its major meetings, and see for myself how the organization conducted itself.

Conferences were not the only yardsticks, but they did provide the perfect setting for evaluating a firm's officers and top distributors. There, I would be able to hear the leaders speak and watch them interact with other people. In fact, I considered that I might even meet a few of the key players face to face. In that way, I figured I would have the opportunity to ask around to see if commission checks and products went out on time. It would also give me a chance to see if they did alien dances on stage with commission checks glued to their foreheads.

Although it wasn't so accurate six or seven years ago, if I were checking into a company today, I'd make sure it was providing 800 numbers for customers and distributors. Phones are a major part of networking, and many MLMs currently are offering national conference calls for business opportunity meetings and to conduct training. These same companies also provide information update lines on products and upcoming events.

Of major consideration in this selection process were the products. I found myself asking this question, "Is this a product that I would sell to my mom and dad or my next door neighbor? Is this a product that I'll use myself and want to tell other people about?"

Common sense dictates that no matter how good a company's marketing plan, if the products or services have no value, the company won't be around for long. Furthermore, reputable network marketing companies often hold patents on their products. So exclusivity is important for both the buyer and the seller, meaning that the products are available only through the MLM distributor base. In other words, no retail stores.

Another way to test the legitimacy of a company is to see if it belongs to any of the trade associations. The best companies are usually members of the Direct Selling Association (DSA) or the Multi Level Marketing International Association (MLMIA). These organizations maintain high standards for their members. At the DSA functions I've attended, I was always impressed by the manner in which leaders of different organizations went out their the way to help one another and share information.

Considering that about 85 percent of all new MLM companies go belly up in their first five years, and most of those in their first 18 months, it's probably wise to get involved with one that has a proven track record. If you're taking a look at a public company, all you have to do is get a Dun & Bradstreet report or ask for an annual report from the company. For private companies, check with the Better Business Bureau or the state attorney general's office.

I did all of these things and more in my search for a MLM that matched up best with me. I traveled to national and regional conferences in Florida and Georgia, taking Karen with me whenever possible, and popped so many opportunity tapes about the companies I was considering into my VCR that it went on the blink.

In the end, it was a product that attracted me to the company I joined. I met with a fellow by the name of Mike Williams who put me on a weight-loss product manufactured by Reliv International, a nutritional food science company headquartered in St. Louis. At the time, I was 25 pounds overweight and in love with double-stuffed Oreo cookies. I'd tried everything but liposuction to get rid of the fat, but nothing worked.

Mike had incredible faith in the Reliv products, and told me if they didn't work, he'd give me my money back. I figured I had nothing to lose. Mike saw or called me nearly every day for a month. In less than two months, I lost the weight and found myself telling other people how I did it.

During that time, I investigated Reliv and found it to be a solid company. By good fortune, I met the president and founder, Bob Montgomery, who had been a very successful businessman before he started Reliv. In our conversations, I appreciated his honest replies to my questions and concerns. But more than that, I sensed that he cared how I felt, and could see that he had deep family values. In fact, that may have been the clincher for me, because I really liked that.

After meeting Bob, I was introduced to Carl Hastings, a highly respected food scientist with a Ph.D. from the University of Illinois, and the executive vice president of the Reliv team. Like Bob, in his warm soft-spoken manner, Carl exuded confidence in a way a person does when he is in love with his work and has nothing to prove.

After meeting with Bob and Carl, I had the opportunity to spend time with Ted Kalogris, a Ph.D. microbiologist, who can count among his many achievements more than a dozen patents. It was he who invented the patented formula for Reliv's nutritional supplement, Classic, the product on which the entire company was based. Being with him was like sitting next to Santa Claus and discovering that the guy wearing the white beard was really Albert Einstein. In our very first conversation, I discovered that this man's main concern in life was helping people. Making money didn't even come in a close second.

Like most people, I've laughed at lawyer jokes and have told one or two on occasion. But when I had the chance to talk with Stephen Merrick of the Chicago firm Fishman & Merrick, one of the Reliv directors, I was impressed. Not only was he a third-generation attorney and the number one graduate of his law class at Northwestern University, his reputation was impeccable.

To say I was sold would be an understatement. Good products, good people, and a good compensation plan. The thrill of finally connecting to the company I wanted to be with wasn't even dampened by the reaction of my colleagues at the Sentinel. They thought I was nuts to give up a job in which I obviously had a great future for something so risky as selling a food supplement out of the trunk of my car. But it didn't take me long to know that I had found a home in multi-level marketing. Now all I had to do was figure out how to build it.

Chapter 5

Common Folk Earning Uncommon Money

"Wealth is not his that has it, but his that enjoys it."
                                        — Benjamin Franklin

I n the beginning, an MLM marketing plan can be a bit intim-
idating. I'll never forget the first time I saw one. A funny
fellow wearing a nice suit stood at the front of a meeting
room and drew a bunch of circles on a white board and put numbers
in them. It was so darn confusing I felt like I was back in my high
school algebra class.

Then he talked about breakaway legs, personal volumes, exponential growth, downlines, uplines and sidelines. I didn't understand a word. I felt like I was back in my high school French
class.

"Do you understand any of this?" I remember asking Karen.

"Not a bit," she whispered. "But I sure like that guy's suit."

We were about to slip out the back door, when the speaker asked
for people to come up and share their stories. That's when I heard
my first income testimonials.

"I've been doing this business for six months and I've never
had so much fun in my life," a young woman blurted into a mike.
"Working part time, I made a little more than $3,000 last month.
I love it."

That got my attention.

Next was a little guy with a chubby face.

"I drove a truck for 20 years," he said. "I was never home. Now, I earn more in a month than I used to earn in a year, and I'm home with my family."

That put me on the edge of my seat.

Most of my adult life, I had dreamed of working out of my home, being my own boss, and watching my children grow up. Now, right in front of me, were people doing just that. What's more, they weren't superhumans oozing with sales skills, but rather common folks like Karen and me. That's what I saw, ordinary people, banding together, helping one another to achieve their dreams.

Most had not started with lots of money. Some of them had struggled even more than Karen and I. But there they were, black and white, educated and uneducated, rich and poor, man and woman, all working together.

One couple talked about doing the business together and how it had drawn them closer. I gave Karen's hand a little squeeze.

"If these people can do this, then we can, too," I remember telling her. "This is the vehicle we've been looking for."

We didn't sign up with that company. The people were great but the product line wasn't for us. However, those folks did convince us that the network marketing revolution was real. Now, all I had to do was figure out how those crazy marketing plans worked.

Surprisingly, once I started studying MLM plans, I quickly realized how simple they really were. Think of it like this. The company pays you for getting it customers, and for teaching other people to do the same. There are three basic ways to make money: retail, wholesale and overrides.

To make retail money, you build a base of customers and sell them products. If you are buying your product at a wholesale price of say 45 percent from your company, you make a 45 percent profit when you make a sale to one of your customers. If it's a $100 sale, you put $45 in your pocket.

When working for someone else, you have to wait until the end of the week, or maybe even two weeks before getting paid. Not so for networkers. For them, every day can be a payday.

I recall Karen coming up to me one morning when I was still fairly new in my networking business.

"Honey, I need a new Easter dress," she asked in her sweetest voice, holding up a very familiar frock. "My old one doesn't look good on me anymore."

"I think you look fantastic," I quickly answered. "That's still a beautiful dress and those holes and frayed ends only give it character."

I could tell by the way that she grabbed me by the throat and stuck a finger in my eye that she wasn't going for it.

"OK, OK, honey," I said as I fought for air. "Why don't you go out and retail some product and you can keep any profits you make today to buy new clothes." Under my breath, I chuckled to myself. "Maybe she'll sell enough to buy a scarf."

"Are you sure?" she asked with a smile.

"Of course, I'm sure," I said. Suddenly I wasn't. There was something about that smile.

You can imagine my amazement when I returned home later that day to find our bed covered with not one new dress, but several. Also, there were two new pairs of shoes and a bathing suit.

"What the heck is all of that stuff ?" I asked Karen when I found her in the bathroom testing a new perfume.

"Oh, that's stuff I bought today," she said with that same smile that had worried me earlier.

"But, honey..."

"Don't but honey me," she said. "You told me I could keep any profits I made. So I went out and sold $600 worth of weight-loss products and then went shopping."

Staggered as I was by her triumph, I did learn a few things from that experience. For starters: watch what I say to my little entrepreneur about what she could do with our profits. Two: I figured there must be thousands of women like Karen who, when properly motivated, could do the same thing. Three: there was serious money to be made retailing good products through people you know, which is exactly what Karen did. Four: she looked stunning in her new Easter dress.

The second way you can make money in MLM is by selling products wholesale. Simply put, this means selling products to distributors that you have recruited into the business. When I sponsored my sister, Nancy, into Reliv, I was at the highest discount level, 45 percent. She was new so her discount level was 25 percent. When I sold Nancy products, I made a 20 percent wholesale profit.

However, the more products Nancy sold to her customers and distributors, the higher her discount level became. In less than 30 days, Nancy and her organization of distributors sold more than $5,000 worth of products. That volume placed her at the 45 percent level, too. In Reliv, we call that level master affiliate.

Now, I could no longer make wholesale profit selling products to Nancy. At that point, Nancy became a breakaway leg. I know it sounds painful, but believe me it really isn't.

In fact, it's when distributors begin to breakaway that the fun and big bucks begin. It's called overrides, which is the third way of making money in network marketing. Overrides are the percentages a distributor receives from the monthly volume of his or her breakaway legs.

When Nancy broke away from me, she became a first level, which I overrode 5 percent. If she did $5,000 in volume selling products to all of her customers and distributors who aren't yet master affiliates, I'd make $250 dollars. Nancy sponsored my mother and father. They are Nancy's first level and my second. My mother and father also are master affiliates at the highest discount level. If mom and dad do $5,000 in volume, Nancy earns $250, and because they are a second level to me, I make 4 percent profit, or $200. Through its Ambassador program, Reliv pays down six levels in this fashion, thus the term multi-level marketing.

The plan that I just described is called the stairstep-breakaway. In my opinion, it is the plan that offers the greatest potential for making the most money. Companies such as Reliv, Amway, Shaklee, Nu Skin, Rexall, Watkins, Discovery Toys and many more use this plan. According to Leonard Clements of *Market Wave,* nearly 90 percent of all MLM companies more than seven years old use the stairstep-breakaway.

There are, however, two other popular plans in the industry. One is called the matrix, and the other is called the unilateral. As a general rule, the matrix plans have limits on how many front-line distributors you can sponsor. The stairstep-breakaways do not. And while the unilateral plans don't limit width, they usually don't pay down as far as the stairstep-breakaway plans.

Needless to say, there are advantages and disadvantages to each. The key is to thoroughly understand the company's plan that you are taking a look at, and see if it best suits your needs and abilities.

Because I wanted to make a fortune, the stairstep-breakaway system had the most appeal, because it allowed me to build a larger downline and draw commissions from a greater number of levels. The stairstep-breakaway offered me unlimited width in my top level, meaning that I could sponsor as many people as I wanted on my frontline, where my sister, Nancy, was. In other words, I could have as many Nancys as I could find and those Nancys could have as many mom-and-dad combinations as they could find, and so forth. Even if the depth was only four or five levels deep, building wide would still create an enormous downline.

The downside for the stairstep-breakaway system is that it is the hardest to work. But I didn't care. I had been working hard for years, and didn't have much to show for it, because I was working for someone else. The reason that it is a more difficult system is that most of the big money comes from the back-end or the deeper levels, which only emerge after you've created a number of break-aways. Obviously, that means that you have to work long and hard before you start seeing any significant money. In addition, most stairstep-breakaways require high monthly volumes. So this system is best for dedicated network marketers who have vision and are willing to delay the jackpot dollars.

The matrix system is like the stairstep-breakaway and the uni-level systems in that it limits your depth, which is the number of levels on which you can be paid. But unlike the other plans, the matrix also limits your width, which is the number of folks on your frontline. Any recruits you bring into a matrix over and above the number allowed on your frontline (usually two to four) spill over into your lower levels. Ultimately, this means that you could sit in a matrix and do nothing, waiting for a high-achiever to build your downline through spillover. In a stairstep or unilevel system, you might have 50 frontline distributors to manage. In a matrix, you might have a maximum of four frontliners. This system, which is easier to explain because there are no breakaways, often attracts individuals who lack the spunk to vigorously pursue their dreams.

As already explained, the unilevel system is like the stairstep-breakaway in that it has unlimited width. The best part of this plan is that it does not allow breakaways so that you can maintain your personal volume. The downside is that depth of a unilevel is pretty shallow, which limits your commission potential severely.

In addition to making money through retail, wholesale and commissions, most companies offer hefty bonus programs for top distributors. These programs can come in the form of cash bonuses, exotic trips and even cars. If you're serious about making it in network marketing, go for the bonus money when you first get started. It could well make the difference between success and failure.

My second month in the business, I was fortunate enough to earn a $3,500 bonus check from Reliv. Karen and I had never seen so much money at one time. We were so excited that we splurged and bought a video camera. My hand trembled when I wrote the check. "Is this a wise thing to do?" I remember thinking to myself.

Today those early videos of my family are worth more to me than all the gold in Fort Knox. I cherish those memories captured by the first gift that network-marketing gave me. There would be many more to come, but I had to see the forest before the individual trees. I had to see the big picture, and pick out the elements that made it big.

Chapter 6

Painting The Big Picture

"We have always held to the hope, the belief, the conviction that there is a better life, a better world, beyond the horizon."
—Franklin D. Roosevelt

The temptation here is to use a fishing simile because selling is like that sport in at least one way. If a prospect isn't biting, then you have to change your bait. Which is simple and true, but far too limiting for those who want to become stars in network marketing.

In sales talk, it's called finding the customer's hot button. In MLM lingo, it's discovering what people want, and then helping them obtain it. The key word here is "helping," and distributors who learn how to do that are the ones destined to become luminaries in the industry. What gives them that instructional ability is really not all that complicated. They look at the trees, then they look at the forest and then they look at the trees again, because it is only when they understand what's really in the big picture that they can pass the information on.

How? Well, they paint the same scene they themselves have absorbed, but now they know where the trees grow, the soil conditions, the topography, the streams that have to be bridged, and all those elements that make up a striking landscape that anyone can understand and enjoy.

In repainting this picture, you can draw attention to all the things that network marketing has to offer since we know that our landscape is packed with all sorts of incredible scenes. In going over the landscape, you never quite know which of those components will capture someone's attention.

For instance, right in the middle of the canvas is the tallest of all the trees, the one marked freedom. Talk about an eye catcher. With MLM, that's the giant sequoia for many of us, because from the top of that big redwood you can see yourself owning your own company and being your own boss.

Get the picture: No more rush-hour traffic, no more alarm clocks waking you up in the morning. Now, you can get the snuggle alarm, which is what I call it when the kids jump in bed with Karen and me for their morning kisses.

Professional networkers don't have mean bosses telling them when they can take their vacations. Nor do they have those time-clock watchdogs giving them the evil eye if they're late from lunch. And you can forget about the fashion police. In network marketing, you wear what you want. Within reason, of course.

Since most networkers work out of their homes, if they feel the need to be at work at 8:30 in the morning, they can step out of the shower at 8:29. Forget about the Sunday afternoon doldrums dragging you down because Monday morning is lurking around the corner. Most networkers don't even know what day of the week it is half the time.

As the CEO of your own company, you call the shots. That way, if you want to coach a Little League team, be a reader at your child's school, or get more involved with your church, you can. You decide who you want to work with and when you want to work.

I'll never forget taking a bunch of kindergarten kids on a field trip to a Christmas tree farm near Eureka, Missouri, in 1995. The little boys were amazed to see a dad driving on a school outing. They were also delighted, as was my younger daughter, Ashley.

''My daddy doesn't have to work anymore,'' I overheard her tell one of her girlfriends. ''He's a Reliv distributor.''

Perfect. A 5-year-old artist painting the MLM picture. Ashley will make a dandy distributor one day.

Then there's the financial scene. I love that part of the painting, because that's where you can find the acorn-and-oak game plan. For those who don't care about the heights of a redwood, but love the strength of oak, this is it. This is where ordinary folks like you and me have a shot at hitting it in a substantial manner. Usually for the price of a kit, and armed with desire and a solid work ethic, you can create a distribution network, one that can provide a residual income for you and your family for the rest of your life.

Can you see yourself living in a beautiful home atop a hill, driving nothing but the finest cars, sending your kids to the best schools and actually being able to retire one day? No more hassles about bills and charge cards pushed to the max. I've been poor and I've been rich. Rich is better, a lot better.

Wealth isn't just money, of course. Indeed, perhaps the greatest treasures are the friendships you develop with the people in your organization. Let's put a cabin in our landscape surrounded by Christmas trees, because that's what the friendships are like. The average networker will acquire more friends in a couple of years than most people will in a lifetime. Dale Carnegie liked to say that "you can make more friends in two months by becoming interested in other people than you can in two years by trying to get other people interested in you."

Not only will you create new friends, but the nature of the business will bring old friends and family members back into your life, like it is around the holidays. That's what happened with me and my best friend, Larry Garner, of Kennesaw, Georgia. Larry and I grew up in Central Florida, and played football and baseball together in high school. Then life and work separated us. Reliv brought us back together.

The fun we have had doing this business could fill this book. Taking trips, going to conferences, prospecting for customers and building our dreams together brought us closer than ever before.

We're on the same team again and it's wonderful. Larry's friendship alone has made my venture into the world of MLM a huge success.

The same is true with my mom and dad, Ann and Tom Pinnock, of Altamonte Springs, Florida. Well into their 70s, my parents have built a wonderful network. Like Larry, they, too, are successful Reliv distributors. Now, when I go to big meetings or conferences, I look forward to seeing my folks there.

Most people their age have been put out to pasture. Not my mom and dad. They are having the time of their lives traveling the world, acquiring new friends, doing presentations, and making a terrific income. They're the absolute best, and I'm very proud of them.

Indeed, my folks never quit growing, and that's a part of the painting that is critical. Network marketing demands personal growth. So, in a way, we're all kind of like trees in that landscape. They'll be some redwoods, some oaks and a lot of Christmas trees, but each one is growing. To be good in this industry, you must become the best person you can be. The fact is, when you deal with people every day, you learn much about yourself and about the strengths and weaknesses of others.

When I first moved to Atlanta, I met a delightful woman by the name of Mindy Jones. She was a people person with enormous potential. But Mindy had a problem; she was terrified of talking in front of large groups of people.

In Art Williams' book *Pushing Up People*, this giant in network marketing writes about how important it is to praise, and encourage your people to achieve excellence. Taking what he had to say as a cue, I decided to push Mindy by scheduling her to speak in front of 50 people. She agreed to give it a go. But on the night of her presentation, she froze with fear.

"Tom, I'll write you a check for a thousand dollars if you'll do this meeting for me," she pleaded. Mindy had plenty of money, and I knew she was serious so I took the check. You see there are many ways to make money in MLM. Just kidding.

"You can do it, Mindy," I said. "You're going to be great."

She wasn't great, but she showed enormous courage in facing her fear. The next time, it wasn't nearly as difficult for her. In less than a year, she was one of the most powerful trainers in all of Reliv.

Eventually, Mindy went to Australia and played a major role in opening up that country to the Reliv products, which created an enormous amount of wealth for her and for me, too. Encouraging people to grow, pushing them out of their comfort zones, and then watching them soar to new heights is one of the most appealing parts of the network-marketing picture.

Then there's travel. You see, our landscape even has coconut palms. How would you like to journey to various parts of the the United States and maybe even the world as an ambassador for your company? Is that a picture in which you can see yourself?

In the past several years, Karen and I have sailed about Australia and Maui. Hiked up mountains in New Zealand and sunbathed on the beaches of Cancun. We've explored the ancient civilizations of Greece, and the pyramids of Mexico. We've taken the trolleys in San Francisco, and surfed the Pacific at San Diego. We've ridden horses through the deserts of Arizona and swam with thousands of colorful fish in the Bahamas. And more, much more.

Furthermore, the company picked up the tab. Reliv President Bob Montgomery likes to say that spoiling his top performers is one of the best parts of his job. What a company! What an industry!

There are a lot of hams in this world who would love to be a star, signing autographs and getting their pictures taken with adoring fans. Well, in our landscape that's one of the scenes, because this is an industry filled with bright lights, towering stages and many stars.

It's only fitting. Top athletes are honored as are actors and other entertainers. Well, multi-level marketing is an industry packed with millions of people all around the world. It is an industry that thrives on recognition of its best performers and goes out of its way to pay tribute to them at spectacular conferences. I heard a journalist once describe a Mary Kay meeting as part-conference and part-*Hello, Dolly!*.

The fact is, if you make it big in this industry, you can count on being on stage, in videos, on radio and featured in magazines and books. Try getting near Dexter Yager at an Amway conference. Look for a major crowd at a Nu Skin meeting and maybe you'll get a glimpse of Mark Yarnell. Go to a Reliv conference and watch as hordes of people flock around top Reliv distributors such as Tom Moody or Joe and Carol Felger. These folks are bigger than life. They've made it to the top and everyone wants to know how. They want to be near them, and have their pictures taken with them. It's a blast.

In Reliv, getting healthy and fit is a big part of that painting. Let's face it, you can have all of the success in the world, but if you don't have your health, it won't mean much. Eating right and exercising are a big part of the Reliv culture. Americans are the most overweight, undernourished people to ever inhabit this planet. To most Americans, the three main food groups seem to be Taco Bell, Burger King and Kentucky Fried Chicken.

More government health insurance programs aren't the answer to the trillion-dollar, health-care crisis in America. The answer is for people to start becoming more responsible for their own health. That means putting the right fuel into their bodies and exercising on a regular basis. Remember, good health isn't a sprint, it's a marathon. If we want to be full of life and energy when we're 75 years old, we'd better starting work on it today.

The last few strokes on this multi-level marketing masterpiece of ours concern worthwhile causes. Those are the fruit trees in this landscape, the part in which we share the bounty. You see, top companies in this industry make a practice of giving something back to the community. For example, Shaklee has taken a keen interest in environmental issues. In 1992, the company initiated a nationwide "make time to make a difference" program, in which distributors did everything from cleaning the shores of local lakes and rivers to recycling used batteries.

Amway is one of the founding corporate sponsors of the Aspen Global Change Institute, which was formed in 1990 to study global change and develop educational materials and outreach programs to inform the public about environmental issues. This awareness and concern stretches around the globe, because Amway affiliates in Asia and Europe also support environmental education and preservation.

Through the Ted Kalogris Foundation, Reliv has been instrumental in getting nutritional foods to undernourished people around the world. The company, along with thousands of distributor volunteers, have lent a hand in all kinds of disasters. They were there with food, drink and volunteers after Hurricane Andrew ripped through South Florida. They helped to man the sandbag lines during the great flood that crippled the St. Louis area in the summer of 1993. And they have sent tons of food into Africa, Haiti and other areas of the world where people were suffering.

Successful network-marketing companies not only help people in time of crisis, but they also have a volunteer army of distributors scattered about the world to help. It's powerful, and getting involved in the world we live in is part of the culture of most good MLM companies.

As you can see, there are plenty of great scenes in this painting. Chances are your prospects are going to like at least one of them, maybe all of them. So use big strokes, plenty of color and lots of stories. Listen and observe carefully as you paint. That way, you'll know what part of the picture the people you are talking to are most interested in. Who knows, with a little practice you might even become a great landscape artist like Thomas Hart Benton or George Caleb Bingham.

Chapter 7

Believe In Yourself

*"We all have possibilities we don't know about. We can do
things we don't even dream we can do."*   —Dale Carnegie

One of the first pitfalls to look out for when you start your
MLM career are the gutter people. They are the little
stinkers in your life who want to pop your balloon. As
Zig Ziglar would say, they are full of "stinking thinking."

You know the ones I'm talking about. What's worse, sometimes
they're in your own family. They're the ones who will put you
and your company down.

"MLM, are you kidding me?" they snorted. "Why that's nothing but an illegal pyramid."

That hurts, but it can get worse.

"You couldn't make any money doing that in a million years,"
people told me. "You're a writer, you don't know anything about
building a business or selling."

The fact is the world is full of negative people who don't believe
in you, your company or your dreams. Furthermore, they don't
want you to be successful. The gutter people want you right where
you are, or lower if that's possible.

A new distributor came up to me in St. Louis not long ago with
tears in her eyes. She told me that her husband was giving her a
hard time about her business.

"He makes fun of what I'm doing," she said in between sobs. "He says I'm not organized and I don't have what it takes."

Standing before me was this charming woman with incredible warmth and caring. I could only pray to one day be as nice a person as she was. Part-time, she was making about a thousand dollars a month and having the time of her life. She was growing, had many new friends, and was a major success in my eyes. And her own husband, probably jealous over her excitement and frightened by her growth, was tearing her down.

I put my hands on her shoulders and looked into her eyes. "You're doing a wonderful job," I told her, "and I'm very proud of what you've accomplished."

She walked away feeling better, but I was struck with a sense of helplessness, because I knew from experience what she was enduring. It was not my place to interfere in a family situation, but if her husband had been there, I might have been able to tell him that if he encouraged her, respected what she was doing, and became her biggest fan, she would probably love him like never before. If he didn't do those things, he would be the gutter person in her business life, and would only make difficult those things that should be a joy for both of them.

I'll have to admit that I don't care much for the gutter people of the world. There are just too many of them. Instead, I like to surround myself with the fountain people. These are the rare folks who bubble over with excitement when you share your success with them.

They have the ability to encourage you, support you, and most importantly, to believe in you. I search for these positive people. I run from the negative ones, who I feel are a cancer in the business and in my life.

Karen was my fountain. When I told her that I wanted to give MLM a go, she didn't throw dirty gutter water on my dream. Instead, she encouraged me.

"Darling, if you think you can do it, then I know you can," she told me. "Just let me know what I can do to support you."

I can't begin to tell you what her support meant to me. In fact, I wouldn't have been successful without it. Too often I see spouses who aren't supportive of their mates. When that happens, I know their road will be a tough one.

Do you remember when you were a child? In those early years, we felt like we could do anything, be anything.

My 6-year-old, Ashley, told me not long ago that she wanted to be an actress when she grows up, and a ballerina, and an artist.

"I'm going to play hockey for the St. Louis Blues after that," she said. "And, of course, I'm going to sell Reliv, too."

I smiled and gave her a big hug.

"Keep dreaming, little princess," I told her. "You can do anything you set your mind to."

Henry Ford put it this way. "Whether you think you can or think you can't — you are right."

The problem is that as we grow older, we start giving up on our dreams and ourselves. Too many gutter people seep into our lives and start telling us what we can't do instead of what we can do. The first step in this business of being your own boss is that you must believe that you can do it.

After all, if you don't believe you can build a distribution network, how in the world are you going to get others to believe in you? I've seen people of all walks of life achieve great success in this industry. Men, women, educated, uneducated, black, white, rich, poor, young and old. If they can do it, so can you. Remember, your own determination to succeed is more important than any other one thing. That was my motivation.

Chapter 8

Believing In MLM

"This most misunderstood concept is revolutionizing marketing and sales the world over."
—John Milton Fogg, editor of *Upline*

I'm proud to be a part of the network-marketing industry. It's a growing revolution made up of millions of people around the world who are striving for freedom and a better way of life. In the United States alone, networkers are moving more than $15 billion worth of products a year, marketing everything from vitamins to automobiles and from vacuum cleaners to phone service.

In spite of the incredible growth of the industry and its ever-increasing respectability, there are still those who give me that funny look before asking in a leery voice, "Is Reliv one of those pyramid schemes?"

I can't help but smile when I hear that question. "Of course it is," I answer. "I wouldn't be involved in anything else."

However, I must admit that the word "scheme" drives me bananas, because network marketing is really a well-established system of doing business, and scheme indicates something nefarious. Still, I have to remind myself to be patient with the question, because it's the same one I used to ask myself when I was a word merchant.

It's not so much that people don't like network marketing as it is that they don't understand it. As networkers, it's our job to educate people about the industry, to treat it with dignity and to strive to be honest and professional in our dealings.

Where the word "scheme" raises the hairs on the back of my neck, the comparison with a pyramid always tickles me. That's because pyramids are made up of blocks supporting one another. Businesses are made up of people supporting one another. There are certainly different ways to market products and reward the sales force, but all business works off the same principle. Someone makes a product, someone sells it, and someone buys it.

When you consider it, even General Motors is a pyramid. The chairman makes money off the efforts of his senior vice presidents, who in return make money off the efforts of their vice presidents. The vice presidents are paid according to the success of their regional and district managers, who in turn are rewarded by the efforts of the car and truck dealers. The dealer makes money off the individuals who sell cars directly to the customers. Oh yes, and the salesman gets a piece of the action, too. Obviously, there's a lot of gold making its way up that pyramid.

Network marketing is the same except there aren't all those middlemen, and, therefore, there is more room at the top in the elephant-dollar category for high achievers. The reality is that few of us will ever be the chairman of General Motors, because in corporate America, there is room for only one chairperson in each company.

In network marketing, a person can come in at the bottom as a new distributor, and go all the way to the top. Not only can he or she make more money than the executives for the company with which he is associated, but he can help other distributors to do the same. In fact, by the very nature of the business, you can't be successful unless you help others to succeed, too. Race, sex, and education are not important. Hard work and determination are.

Today, I smile whenever I see a pink Cadillac going down the street. I know that the driver is a successful Mary Kay distributor, an entrepreneur like myself. She is helping women to look more beautiful and is teaching others how to build a business that can be managed out of the home.

My wife's Mary Kay representative is Rose Monsyk of Washington, Missouri. A delightful person well into her second decade with the company, Rose is a thoughtful and caring individual who provides my bride with wonderful products and terrific service. For Karen's part, she likes buying from Rose because she wants to support someone she knows and cares about. To our way of thinking, Rose is a great alternative to Karen's other choice, which would be to drive to the mall, and buy products from a stranger.

In her book, *Mary Kay, You Can Have It All,* Mary Kay Ash writes that "my motivation for going into business was to help women. I wanted to provide opportunities for them to create better lives. I saw Mary Kay Cosmetics as a vehicle for women to realize their dreams."

Mary Kay Ash and her legions of beauty consultants sell more than a billion dollars worth of cosmetics annually. That's a lot of dreams.

Sometimes, when you tell people that you're in a network-marketing company they say, "You mean like Amway?"

"You bet," I answer with enthusiasm. "Amway's a great company."

In fact, all networkers owe a word of thanks to the founders of Amway, Jay Van Andel and Rich DeVos. As mentioned earlier in this book, these two high school buddies paved the way for the rest of us when they founded their company in 1959 and, in effect, opened up careers for more than two million independent Amway distributors in 54 nations and territories around the world. Today, Amway's annual sales come in at about $5 billion.

In his book *Compassionate Capitalism*, DeVos writes: "In looking back, we don't measure our success first in billions of dollars. We measure it in remaining true to our dream. All along we wanted to own our own business."

Because of Amway's enormous success, many think it is the granddaddy of all network marketing companies. Not true. There are a number of others that predate it, including Nutrilite Products, Inc. Which was founded in 1941 by Carl Rhenborg

Rhenborg came up with the idea of recruiting independent distributors to sell his food supplements because he was short of start-up capital. It was a novel idea at the time, allowing him to operate with little overhead and no salaries. In addition, he didn't have to pay commissions until after the sales had been made.

But his plan wasn't all one way. He concocted a system whereby his distributors would earn from what they sold themselves, but also gain commissions off the people they recruited and trained. Obviously, the more people they recruited and trained, the more money they made. Sound familiar? Of course it does, because what was off-beat in 1941 is standard operating procedure today.

With this system, the little guy could now make money off his or her own efforts, plus the efforts of others, just like big business. Once an organization of distributors and customers were in place, the networkers could enjoy the fruits of their labor in the form of residual income. If you guessed that Van Andel and DeVos got their start in network marketing with Nutrilite, you're right on the button. They just improved on what they learned.

Van Andel and DeVos weren't the originators of the concept, but they were pioneers, and they should get their due. In fact, it's important for networkers to be champions of the industry, to speak well of the good companies and people in it. To elevate the opinion of multi-level marketing, it's essential that networkers support one another and not fall into the ugly habit of running down other companies. When we do that, we're communicating that it must be a lousy industry if it has only one good company.

Take the time to read Richard Poe's excellent book, *Wave 3: The New Era In Network Marketing*. Then reach for Debbi Ballard's book, *How to Succeed in Your Own Network Marketing Business*. In addition to these works, there are also a number of publications available to help you better understand network marketing. Leonard Clements, publisher of *MarketWave,* John Milton

Fogg, editor of *Upline,* and Corey Augenstein, publisher of *Down-Line News* are all champions of network marketing, and you can learn a great deal from them.

It only makes sense to arm yourself with knowledge and respect for this incredible industry. Believe in it with all your heart, and who knows, you may become a leader in this revolution that is altering the face of the marketplace.

The next time someone asks what you do, tell them with pride: "I'm in network marketing, and having the time of my life."

When I'm asked what I market, I answer: "Health and wealth. What would you like to hear about first?"

Chapter 9

Believe In Your Products

"It is not the employer who pays wages — he only handles the money. It is the product that pays wages."
— Henry Ford

Nothing in network marketing is more important than your product. To be successful, you must believe with all your heart that what you're marketing is the best in the world. If you don't believe that, it will be difficult to succeed.

When someone comes to me and says that they want to be a distributor, but that they have no interest in taking my products, I tell them to take a hike. It's not that I'm being mean, it's just that I know that good networkers always believe in what they are selling. After all, if you don't use the product yourself, how in the world can you convince someone else that they need it.

Networkers sell from their hearts. As a rule, most aren't professional salespeople. They are homemakers, truck drivers, teachers, lawyers, firefighters and just about any other thing you can think of. They sell their products to friends and family, whether it's skin care or car wax, because they use it themselves and believe in it.

That's our foundation and power. It works because it is honest. People are not stupid. They can tell if you use and believe in what you are marketing.

So the first step in becoming a strong networker is to use your products and get results. If you're thinking about marketing skin care, and you find that the company's products are making your skin look younger and feeling softer, you won't be able to keep your mouth shut. This is sometimes called "being a product of the product." In other words, if you're 50 pounds overweight, you're probably going to have a tough time convincing someone that you have the best weight-loss product in the world. On the other hand, if people watch you drop 50 pounds, they'll knock your door down in order to buy your products.

The next step is to get other people on the product. I felt pretty good about Reliv's weight-loss program after I shed nearly 25 pounds. I felt even better when Karen lost 15 pounds and my neighbor lost 40 pounds. My dad got on the nutritional supplement and told me that he never felt so good in all his life.

I got more excited about their results than I did my own. You see, networking is a story business, and the more stories you have to share, the stronger you are, and the stronger you are, the bigger your business will be.

One of the benefits in dealing in nutrition and weight-loss is that customers and distributors oftentimes get emotionally tied to the product. I've found that ordinary people who get extraordinary results can be unstoppable. For example, I watched in amazement as Susan Miller of Boston lost 188 pounds in 15 months.

At last check, she had kept the weight off for more than a year. Needless to say, she is emotionally tied to the Reliv products and has no problems telling other people about them. And as you can imagine, everyone she knows wants to know how she did it.

If you're marketing car cleaner, you need to drive the cleanest and shiniest car in town. If you're selling beauty care products, you need to make sure that your lipstick is on straight and that your makeup is fresh. If you're selling toys, then your kids better be playing with them at home.

That's one of the beauties of our industry. We are all consumers of our products. Get enough consumers, and enough distributors consuming and getting consumers, and the next thing you know you have this huge network that's making money for you while you're sleeping. It can happen, so long as you've got a product that you believe in.

Chapter 10

Make A Commitment

"We know how rough the road will be, how heavy here the load will be, we know about the barricades that wait along the track, but we have set our soul ahead upon a certain goal ahead and nothing left from hell to sky shall turn us back."
— Vince Lombardi

T o be successful in life one has to be willing to make a commitment. That is true whether you're talking about a football team, a network-marketing career or a marriage. Dig your heels in, put your blinders on and charge ahead.

Think about it like this. What kind of marriage would you have if you said to your spouse at the beginning of the marriage that you'd only be willing to try it for a few weeks? Not only that, but you were going to keep your eyes open in case someone better came along. Such a marriage would be doomed from the start because of a lack of commitment.

There are a number of critical areas in network marketing that demand commitments in order to be successful. The first concerns your product. If you're selling nutrition, use it. If you don't, you're going to fail.

"Are you taking your nutrition twice a day?" is the first question I ask a struggling distributor. Networkers who aren't faithful to their own products can't expect their customers or downline to be faithful either. Indeed, their lack of faith is as easy to spot as a cheap hairpiece on a windy afternoon.

Next, you must make a commitment to your customers. It is your duty to truly care about them and give them terrific service. In return, they need to promise you that they are going to use your product in order to give it a fair test. Let's face it, no matter how good the product, if it sits on the shelf, it isn't going to work.

You must also make a commitment to the people you sponsor into the business. These recruits must know that you are going to be there for them, that you are going to train them, and that you are going to help them in any way that you can. My sponsor, Mike Williams, made that kind of commitment to me.

"If you ever need me for an appointment anyplace or anytime," he said, "just know that I'll be there five minutes early."

Mike's promise to me didn't come cheap. He made it plain from the start that if he was going to put time into me, he wanted me to make a commitment to him. My end of the bargain was to give Reliv everything I had for at least two years, and during that time, I was never to miss a meeting or training. We remained true to our promise and both of us became successful.

Mike didn't have much education. He told me the only reason he got out of ninth grade was because he had good eyesight. "If the fellow next to me would have applied himself a little more, I could have made more of my life," he used to joke. But what Mike lacked in formal education, he more than made up with passion and commitment.

The final promise needs to be to your company. One of the worst things that can happen in this industry is to become an MLM junkie. Those are the folks who run from one company to the next, always in search of the hottest new opportunity. One day, these folks are talking about how great XYZ company is and the next day they're bad mouthing XYZ, and trying to convince everyone to join PU International.

After a while the MLM junkie loses all credibility and no ones wants to listen to them let alone follow them. The successful networker finds a home and stays put. They understand loyalty and they're not going to be lured away by a pay plan that promises them an extra percent on the fifth level.

I've seen dozens of people make this mistake. In some cases, they were top earners. They chased after greener grass only to end up choking on it. Once you've jumped ship, it's real tough to climb back on board again. More often than not, the ship, filled with your downline, sails on without you.

I've also run across people who think they can do two or more network-marketing companies at the same time. That's nuts. I've yet to meet a top earner in the industry who does that. In this business, as in life, you can have only one lover. To do otherwise will only serve to confuse your downline and set yourself up for disaster.

Think about it this way. If you're in a number of companies, then your downline thinks that's the way it's done and gets in a number of companies as well. They probably won't be the same companies that you're in.

It's hard enough to get your people to attend trainings, meetings, conferences, do parties, and all the other stuff for one company. Do you suppose they can do it for a number of them?

Not only that, but now you've lost your focus, and even worse, so has your downline. Instead of concentrating in one area, they're all out there trying to recruit one another into other companies. It becomes confusing.

I learned this lesson the hard way. When I first got going in Orlando, I had a number of people who were selling Reliv products, and at the same time, water filters for another company. Because I was afraid of losing them, I never said anything about their other activities.

Then it happened. We had a big meeting in Orlando. Reliv President Bob Montgomery, his wife, Sandy, and Executive Vice President Carl Hastings were all there. Moments before the event kicked off, one of the water-filter people dropped tablets into the water pitchers scattered about the room.

The water turned yellow, no doubt showing that the hotel had ample chlorine in its system. The demonstration might have been fine at a water-filter meeting, but not at ours. To make matters worse, they also put up a water-filter display on a back table.

Karen quickly gathered up the filters, but it was too late to do anything about the water. You can imagine my horror when Bob Montgomery asked for something to drink. He took one look at his glass and said with a wink, ''With water like this, you'd better be on our nutrition.''

The water-filter folks left us after that. They got into something else, and now I think they're in PU International. Serves them right.

I've found that in network marketing, as in life, that the happiest people have a sense of commitment in everything they do. It doesn't matter if it's building a business, playing tennis, or coaching a Little League team. In our industry, you will find wonderful people who love what they are doing and will be more than willing to share their commitment with you. It's one of the nicest and most important parts of the business.

Chapter 11

Service With A Smile, And Follow-up

*"The purpose of human life is to serve, and to show
compassion and the will to help others."*
                                        —Albert Schweitzer

T here are two essential ingredients to getting and keeping
customers. Number one, you must have a product that they
want at a fair price. Number two, you must give them the
kind of personal service that you wish someone would give you.

Good service is becoming a lost art. Part of the reason is that
the marketplace has changed so drastically in recent years. Malls
and the super-warehouse stores offering a huge selection of com-
parative products at low prices have had a dramatic effect on
shopping America. Office Depot, Toys R' Us, Sam's Club, Best
Buy, Home Depot and all the rest of the mega-stores do business
differently than the individually owned stores that once made up
the shopping districts of towns and cities.

For years, the little stores survived because they offered topnotch service. The store owners lived in the community. They not
only knew your name, but they also knew the names of your
brothers and sisters. If you had a dog, they often knew its name,
too.

I can still recall all of the business owners of my youth, because
they all played a big part in my life. Mr. Cornell ran the local
garage, and his son, Jamie, was my best friend. When I was ready

to purchased my first car, it was Mr. Cornell who went to work for me to be sure I was getting value for my money.

Just up the street from the Cornell's garage was a small general store owned by Mr. Blackford. The Blackfords lived near my grandparents. Their son, Paul, a terrific running back for Lyman High School, was one of my heroes when I was growing up. After school and on Saturdays, he worked behind the counter at his father's store and, whenever I came in, he always gave me free bubble gum.

Joyce and Davie Sims owned the office supply store that I loved to frequent as a kid. Mrs. Sims knew exactly what kind of folder I needed for my book report, the right ribbon for my old typewriter, and the perfect birthday cards for my older sisters. Their daughter, Karen, and I were playmates. When she and I grew up, we got married.

Mr. Snodgrass, who owned the hardware store, taught me about nails and screws. Sometimes, when I was in need of something and didn't have any money, he'd trade me supplies for empty pop bottles.

The supermarket was owned by a neighbor, Mr. Jabe, whose son, Jerry, was counted among my closest friends. Jerry and just about every other boy in town bagged groceries for his father at one time or another. Usually, it was the first job most of us had, and it was one we took seriously, because if we goofed off, he'd tell our parents.

These same folks were also the ones who sponsored our Little League teams, worked the refreshment stands at the football games and charity events, and helped our families in time of need. They were the business fiber of our community, providing what I later came to recognize as an integral part of a network of family and friends working together and supporting one another.

In most of America, the mom and pop stores exist only in old Norman Rockwell paintings. Like aging actors, they lost their appeal in favor of shiny new malls. And when they could no longer draw a crowd, they retired to barely remembered obscurity. We know they existed mostly because we see and sometimes resent the shells of their past glory on downtown streets, forgetting that those were the places that gave jobs to people we knew.

In our current era, our towns are edged by busy streets and highways lined with strip malls, franchise operations and warehouse stores. We do business with people we don't know. Most often, the owners of these big stores don't even live in our communities.

The salespeople are paid too little and often aren't knowledgeable about their products. Because they have no vested interest in the company for which they work, most employees at the megastores could not care less if we come back or not.

I've never been in one of these stores and had anyone call me by my name. Service is not their game. They deal in low prices. Period.

Low prices aren't all bad, and neither are these stores. But they have created a void, because bigness has a way of depersonalizing things. And getting up close and personal is where networkers can shine. People still want service, and need to know that their business is deeply appreciated.

Good networkers show appreciation by following up on a sale. Years ago, a Scandanavian ice skater named Sonja Heine would glide around the rink after a show shaking hands with people in the front seats. She was saying thank you for coming and paying to see me skate and, at the same time, inviting the audience to do the same thing the following year. Her product was grace and beauty, and she was marketing in a very personal way.

As a networker, we do the same thing with personal service. We are saying thank you for buying our product and, when you need our product again, we'll be here to sell it and provide you with whatever service is required. It's not exactly grace and beauty, but it's in the same neighborhood. After all, our customers are often our friends and neighbors, just like in times past.

It doesn't matter if we're selling nutrition, jewelry, makeup, car wax, cleaning supplies or baskets, our job as a networker is to teach our customers about our products and then to stand behind those products. In most cases, we are ready to follow up to be sure we've given satisfaction, because we know a lifetime customer is a valued commodity.

As good networkers, it's important to be active in our communities, too. It is a part of the industry's culture. To be truly successful, we must get to know people, to network with them, to care about their lives.

In many cases, those of us in multi-level marketing often have the luxury of free time, because we have built a distribution network of consumers, which provides a residual income. Once we've carved out that free time, we can more easily become involved in schools, churches, Little League, Girl Scouts and all sorts of worthwhile programs. If you're a networker, it's important to be involved in your community, because it's good for you and your business.

For example, people in Atlanta are not going to soon forget that a large group of Reliv distributors spent a Saturday not too long ago cleaning and painting a local food shelter. Not only did they spiff it up, they also stocked the empty shelves.

In a more spectacular incident of a networker getting involved and making a difference is Nu Skin distributor Mark Yarnell, who once raised $185,000 for a Michigan woman who was in need for a bone-marrow transplant. Then, at another time, he and his wife, Rene, became the founders of the International Green Cross.

You see, it's not all about making money. It's about making a difference in your community.

Chapter 12

Customers Are The Key

"Think enthusiastically about everything; but especially about your job. If you do so, you'll put a touch of glory in your life. If you love your job with enthusiasm, you'll shake it to pieces." —Norman Vincent Peale

T he day I bought a distributor kit from Reliv for $35, I became a business owner. It was certainly cheaper than buying a McDonald's or a TGI Friday's franchise. Not only that, but I didn't have any employees to worry about, and there were plenty of people willing to teach me the business. For free.

It didn't take long to figure out that if I was going to make any money, I needed to build a customer base. I reasoned that if I could get 25 households to buy my nutritional foods, I would be on my way. They were products that they would buy anyway, but now they would be getting better stuff, and they would be getting them from me. Perfect.

Estimating that the average family would spend about a $100 a month, at 25 customers, at would come out to $2,500 in sales. Not bad. At a 45 percent-profit level, that meant I would be putting $1,125 in my pocket, pretty good part-time money.

Of course, if I wanted to make more money off my efforts, I'd have to get more customers. That's a basic business principle. For your business to make money, you must move goods for a profit. Obviously, the more goods you sell, the more money you make.

The nice thing about dealing in consumable product is that your customers reorder each month. Once you've done your job, and they become loyal customers, they don't demand as much of your time. That allows you the space to get more customers and make more money.

I'll never forget my first two customers. Dad was number one. I went to him because I was aware that no matter what I tried, he would step forward and support my efforts. It was a cinch, and I knew it, but in spite of the certainty of the sale, my sponsor, Mike Williams, came along, too. Good sponsors will do that for their baby distributors. They are their support and protection against someone who might be tempted to nip a new business in the bud.

Dad listened to me talk for 15 minutes about the importance of good nutrition and how great my Reliv products were going to make him feel. He didn't tell me at the time, but later said he was certain that Mike was going to load me up with a bunch of products and head for the hills.

In spite of his misgivings about Mike, Dad bought the first can of nutrition from me. Although I only made $10 on the sale, it felt like a thousand at the time. I knew I could count on him, which is why I went to him first.

My mom, however, never did come downstairs to listen to what I had to say. Dad said she had a terrible headache. I think she was sick at the thought of her oldest son selling nutrition products out of the trunk of his car. But her misgivings would soon be alleviated.

The second person I contacted was Karen's dad, Davie Sims. Like my father, I was sure I could depend on him to try my products. Actually, I knew I had an in because a few weeks earlier, he had told me that he wanted to drop about 10 pounds, and I just happened to have a weight-loss product in my line.

As I walked up to the door with four cans of Ultrim Plus tucked under my arms, Davie was there to meet me.

''What you got there, Tom?'' he asked.

"It's a weight-loss product that Karen and I are selling," I said with plenty of gusto.

A successful businessman, Davie had been in sales most of his life. Like other sales people, he was a perfect target for a pitch because he appreciated entrepreneurs.

When sales people are in your own family, convincing them should require almost no effort. Of course, if you're the kind of person who doesn't remember birthdays, never calls his mom, and is always arguing with someone in the family, you have probably reduced your potential in that market area. Good networkers have healthy relationships with friends and family. And Davie was a mentor and one of my best friends.

"I was hoping you might be willing to help us out by trying this stuff," I said, laying it on the line. Then a grin spread across my face as I offered this challenge: "Who knows, it might even improve your golf game."

Davie didn't hesitate for a second. "I'd be happy to," he said, "especially if it's going to help my golf game. Let me get my checkbook."

He bought $200 worth of products from me that afternoon, which really had me grinning. In less than an hour, I had made nearly $100. Never before had I made that much money in so short a time.

I was on a roll, and as I pulled into my driveway, I noticed Bill, one of my neighbors, mowing his grass. Bill's belly was so big that it was draped over the mower handlebar, and I couldn't wait to tell him about my weight-loss product.

Snatching up a can of the chocolate-flavored Ultrim Plus, I ran next door. "Bill," I said, trying to shout above the whirling sounds of the mower, "Bill, I've got something here that's guaranteed to help you lose weight. It really works! You're going to love it."

Bill looked at me as if I was trying to hand him a parking ticket. Not only did he not bother to turn off the mower, the expression on his face turned angry. "Take your little can and get your butt out of my way," he shouted back. "I don't want any of that junk!"

I was devastated. From being on top of the world five minutes earlier, I went to feeling like a piece of wet crabgrass stuck to the bottom of Bill's stained sneakers. Sagging, I quickly retreated, muttering under my breath. It was my first no and it hurt. It wouldn't be my last, however.

My dad got amazing results on the product and today is a very successful Reliv distributor, too. When Mom saw the effect the products had on Dad, she tried them, too, and gained similar satisfaction. After that, she began telling her friends about her son the genius.

Regarding my father-in-law, he is still one of my best customers, ordering product by the case. Even Bill came around. About a year after the incident on his lawn, he apologized for his rudeness, got on the weight-loss product and dropped nearly 40 pounds.

By the time that Bill became a customer, however, I was well on my way to success in multi-level marketing, and I still credit that to the initial support I received from Dad and Davie. If it hadn't been for them buying those first cans of product from me, perhaps I might have given up and today there wouldn't be hundreds of distributors and customers in my organization.

Building a nice little retail base through family, friends and neighbors may be as far as you want to go with your business. After all, with a nice little customer base, you could make a terrific retail profit, and you would be doing it working part-time. Actually, this is the ultimate goal for many networkers. If that's your goal and you reach it, then you have my congratulations.

Of course, distributors who stop here rely entirely on their own efforts. We call that linear income. To get to the next level of networking, you must begin to leverage the time and efforts of others.

That's where the fun begins, and that's where you can make the most money. Keep in mind that some of your customers are going to want to make additional income as well. That's what happened to Mom and Dad. They loved the Reliv products and, after seeing my success, and my sister Nancy's success, they wanted to get into the business, too. So Nancy sponsored them.

When you sponsor someone into the business, your mission is to teach and help them get customers and distributors. The exciting part is that now you're not only making money on your own efforts and what you personally sell, but also on the efforts of your new distributors.

Now that you have your first distributors, the next step is to simply teach them to do the same thing you did. Their goal is to get customers on the product and to sponsor other distributors to do the same. The more distributors or little businesses you have underneath you, the more money you make. The networker's goal is to get a lot of people doing a little, and then a little more.

A business with 20 or 25 customers is hardly big. There is nothing earth-shattering about selling a couple of thousand dollars worth of products each month, especially when you're dealing in repeat business. But if you teach five people to do this, and they all teach five, and those people teach five, the exponential growth can multiply into hundred of little business in your downline. How long that takes depends on how hard you're willing to work.

Let's say that you develop 200 of these little businesses over a period of several years. Keep in mind that they will pop up all over the country and even the world if your opportunity is international. People know people everywhere. That's the power of networking.

If 200 distributors do $2,000 a month in sales that produces a volume of $400,000. A lot of people doing a little equals a lot. If your override on that volume averages 4 percent, you make $16,000 a month. That's how successful networkers make big money. Granted, it takes time to grow an organization that large, but what else can the average person do that has a similar earning potential?

If you had 100 little businesses in your organization, your override check would be $8,000 a month. Keep in mind that I'm not adding in retail, wholesale, or bonus money. Just overrides. Cut that number to 50, and you will still be making more than $4,000 a month. And remember, that's not you getting 50, that's you getting five who get five, and so on.

J. Paul Getty understood this concept perfectly. Getty, an American executive who built a financial empire in the oil business, had a fortune estimated at $4 billion when he died. When asked how he managed to accumulate so much in one lifetime, he replied: "To be rich, you must be in business for yourself. You must have repeat products. Duplicate your efforts. Guarantee your products. Give better service than the competition and reward those who do the work."

Sounds like network marketing to me.

Chapter 13

Love And Sell Are Four-Letter Words, Too

"Nothing happens until somebody sells something."
— Bob Montgomery

Keep in mind that no matter how you slice it, networking is selling, and selling is not a bad word. In America, and all free-market places, nobody would make any money if it weren't for the sales people moving products. Everything you have — from your house to your watch — is a result of someone selling you something.

One of the reasons some people dislike selling is they hate the idea of being sold. They have visions of high-pressure sales tactics and being taken advantage of. Another reason is that people dread the thought of being turned down and hearing that hideous two-letter word "no."

Truly believing in your products or services will certainly get you over the first hurdle. With a trillion-dollar health-care crisis in America, I feel that I have a moral obligation to share my products. If you know in your heart that you have a product or service that people truly need, you won't have a problem sharing it with others.

And for goodness sakes, don't let a little two-letter word like "no" scare you. Successful networkers learn not to take "no's" personally. They understand that not everyone is going to be interested in their products or in a potential opportunity. That's life. The trick is to keep on talking.

Ironically, the same folks who have trouble selling are the same ones who don't have a problem with buying. In their minds it's OK to spend money but not OK to collect it. Entrepreneurs enjoy collecting money.

Buying is one of the ways that we vote in a free society. When we purchase a product, we are voting for it. If the company gets enough votes, it wins. If it doesn't, it goes out of business. There are plenty of companies that lose elections every year. Its products or service just didn't measure up. Or maybe its sales force was afraid of the word "no."

Many times, when I meet with new people, they tell me that they don't think they can be successful in multi-level marketing because they've never sold anything in their life. That just isn't true. All of us have been in sales.

When you take the time to think about it, you've been selling your whole life, and the chances are you're probably pretty darn good at it. Remember when you were a kid? Back in those days, you sold your folks on why they should buy you a new bike, take you to the mall, or let you spend the night with your best friend.

When you got older, you convinced your girl friend or boy friend to marry you, you sold yourself in order to get that job, you talked the police officer out of giving you the speeding ticket. We sell one another every day.

Life is all about selling. Insurance agents, painters, plumbers, cleaners, dentists and everyone else you can think of only make money when they sell people on what they do.

How many times have you convinced friends to try a restaurant because you liked it? Have you ever recommended a movie or a book to someone because you enjoyed it? Of course you have. The problem is that no one ever sends us a free book or a ticket to the movies because of our efforts. In MLM, you get paid for sharing. It's a blast, and it's easy if you'll just get out of your comfort zone and start talking from your heart.

Oftentimes, it's the people who have never been in sales who are the most successful. Professional sales people can come across as being too slick. MLM is not slick. It should be honest and sincere.

We're not Corporate America. We're just a bunch of regular folks banding together, helping one another and being ourselves. It's OK if your presentations aren't polished and perfect. No one is grading you. You don't have a boss. Just be yourself and sell yourself like you've been doing for years.

A while back, I sponsored a terrific fellow by the name of Tommy Gibson. Tommy, who lives in St. Louis, was a professional salesman who knows more about selling than I ever will. He was technical and his approach came from his brain instead of his heart. He was always looking to close the deal. He was so busy selling that he forgot to be himself.

It took months to get Tommy out of the sales game and into the people business. But once he learned the golden rule of MLM — find out what people want and help them to get it — he became successful. The fact is, regardless of what your product line is, the first thing you must sell in this business is yourself. People will be delighted to supply us with the money we need if we will but serve them and put them first.

Sometimes, people get caught up in sales techniques. But the fact is, even bad techniques work if you talk to enough people. I have a nephew who walked into his second-grade class, took one look at his teacher, and said ''you're fat — you need to call my uncle.'' Even for a second grader, that's poor technique.

The funny thing is that the teacher called me. She wasn't real friendly at first, but I finally got her on my weight-loss product. She ended up losing 32 pounds. Not only that, but she led me to a half dozen other customers. I figured I made about $250 a month in retail profit because of what a 7-year-old had said. I gave him 10 bucks.

When you get right down to it, the best sales technique is your enthusiasm. And your excitement will come from the acronym formed by the last four letters of the word enthusiasm — I.A.S.M. I am sold myself. If you're sold, you can sell the world.

Chapter 14

Communication Is The Key To Success

Two stonecutters were asked what they were doing. The first said, "I'm cutting this stone into blocks." The second replied, "I'm on a team that's building a cathedral."   —Unknown

I f there is one word that best describes network marketing, it would be communication. As networkers, you are paid to tell people about your products and the opportunity afforded by those products. Good communicators tell lots of folks and make lots of money. Bad communicators have trouble convincing their mothers to try their products and end up working evenings at the local supermarket.

It's been my experience, however, that new distributors often talk too much. If you see your neighbors skedaddling out their back door when they see you coming, you're probably overdoing it. If you're the kind that brings out a flip chart at Thanksgiving and starts showing the compensation plan, you probably need help.

To be a good communicator you must first be a good listener. That's why God gave you two ears and one mouth. He expects you to listen twice as much as you talk. Good listeners are worth their weight in gold. They understand that they can never learn anything while they are talking.

The first step in getting a customer or distributor is to sell yourself. The best way to do that is by taking a sincere interest in the other person. People enjoy talking about themselves and their families, and while they're talking, you listen and learn.

Many times, they'll tell you that they're unhappy with their jobs, or that they work too much, or that they don't like their boss, or that they don't have enough money to send their children to college. Such comments give you the perfect lead in to talk about the opportunity available to them in multi-level marketing.

"What do you do?" is a question that I often ask people when I meet them for the first time. Usually, they tell me all about their work. I listen very carefully, never interrupting. When they finish, they usually turn to me and ask, "What do you do?"

"I own my own marketing company," I respond.

"And what do you market?" they ask.

"Health and wealth," I say with vigor. "What would you like to hear about first?"

Never forget that what you say is never as important as how you say it. If you're excited, you'll never go wrong. People are always attracted to people who love what they are doing.

Keep in mind that what you do is often more important than what you say. When I first went to my neighbors back in Longwood, Florida, most of them didn't take me too seriously. Part of the problem was because I talked the ears right off their heads. The other reason, which I didn't know at the time, was that many of them wanted to see if I'd stick with it and have success.

First, they saw me lose weight. Then they saw me get new clothes, a new car, and then heard that Karen and I were buying a new home. At that point, they began approaching us about our career change.

"Could you tell us about that thing you're doing again?" they asked. "We weren't listening the first time."

Besides talking too much, I had another problem when I first started my MLM career. I begged. Believe me, it wasn't very pretty. I'd get down on my knees and plead with people to try my products or get into the business with me. Can you imagine what those people must have been thinking?

"Yep, Tom, I sure would like to do this thing with you. Nothing would please me more than to get down on my knees and beg like you. I can see myself doing that. This is indeed a very attractive opportunity."

It wasn't until I got strong and started showing my products and opportunity some respect that people became interested. Besides, anyone that you have to beg, drag or wrestle into this business isn't worth having. When I got off my knees, so did my business.

When you first get going, it's difficult to explain the products or the compensation plan because you don't know much about them yourself. That's when you grab your sponsor and let them do the communicating for you. There is no better way to learn than listening to real presentations to real prospects.

Now, if you're one of those orphans who doesn't have a local sponsor to help you, or just as bad, your sponsor isn't dedicated, then the next best thing is to use tools. Most good companies provide opportunity videos and audio tapes that you can pass out to prospects. They should also have quality brochures and presentation books that show the product lines and the compensation plan.

The beauty about using these tools is that the presentation is duplicable for your downline. Anybody can stick an opportunity tape into a VCR. Even newspaper reporters can do that.

The first place to start with your service or product is with people you know. Simply make a list of all your friends, all of your spouse's friends, all the people you went to school with, members of your church, neighbors, people you do business with, Little League friends, PTA buddies, friends of friends, children's friends, people you get Christmas cards from, people you should send Christmas cards to, friendly clerks and anyone else you can think of. When you're finished, you should have at least 200 names. If you communicate properly and work hard with your people, that's all you'll ever need.

We call this list your center or circle of influence. It could be worth a fortune to you. And don't give me that guff about not wanting to sell to friends and family. Remember, you've picked a

company with terrific products, you're going to give them excep-
tional service, and there's an incredible opportunity to make
money.

You're talking about a gold mine here, and the first people you'd
better share it with are your friends and family. If you don't think
that way, you probably don't feel too strongly about your products
or opportunity. If that's the case, you'd better call the manager of
your local supermarket and see if you can get a job there. As for
me, I'd much rather buy something from a friend or family member
than go to the mall and give my money to a stranger.

Most of my business was built through my center of influence.
I brought in people I knew and loved and I worked hard for them.
Tom Moody, a top Reliv distributor in Chicago, did the same
thing. He sponsored two of his uncles, Jim and Pat Rogers, both
of whom are extremely successful today. So is his cousin, Shawn
Burgeron. They are a family team and they have a ball doing the
business together.

Keep in mind that each time you bring someone into your
business, you are now into their center of influence, or their list of
200 names. When you sign someone up off that list, you are now
into their center of influence and so on. It's truly the best way to
do the business and, if done properly, it can provide a never-ending
source of leads.

That list, by the way, is not a straight line that can be trashed
once you've gone through it. It is really a circle. Perhaps someone
on the list, who wasn't interested a year ago, suddenly finds himself
without a job. Now, the timing is right for them to hear about your
opportunity. It only makes sense to ask people who give you one
of those dreaded ''no's'' if it's OK to get back with them a few
months down the road.

''Just want to let you know how I'm doing,'' is a great thing to
say. They'll always say yes. No one likes to say no, especially
twice in a row.

You'll always be adding to your list as well. Networkers are
always meeting new people and remembering old ones. Make a
list and start setting appointments. And you'd better do it before
someone else signs them up. You never know, it might even be
me.

Chapter 15

Working The Cold Market

*"I'm a great believer in luck, and I find the harder I work
the more I have of it."*   — Thomas Jefferson

O K, so you don't have a center of influence and the folks
that you do know told you to take a hike. Or maybe you
don't believe in yourself enough to go to your friends
and family. Or perhaps you just moved into a new town and don't
know anyone.

I'll have to admit that I get a bit nervous when a new distributor
tells me that she's worked on her list for three days and only has
two people on it, and only one of those likes her. As a rule of
thumb, a person with no friends usually isn't cut out for networking. But not always, so long as she's teachable.

One of my favorite stories of a networker who built his business
in a cold market is John Quirk, of Atlanta. John arrived at my new
house one afternoon in a car that was so awful it made my old van
look good. It huffed and puffed up my driveway, backfired a
couple of times, coughed up a cloud of black smoke, gave one last
sigh, and then poured out a couple of quarts of oil all over my
drive.

A few moments later, John popped out of the cloud of smoke
and apologized for the black puddle. He had answered a newspaper
ad. Like all ads, you never know what you're going to get.

John and I went inside the house and sat at my kitchen table. He told me that he had $64 to his name, no job and a son, Sean, that wanted to go to the University of Michigan. He also said that he didn't have a warm market because he had lived in Atlanta only a short time.

"This isn't going to be easy," I remember telling him. "You're going to have to work harder than you've ever worked in your life."

"I know that," he answered with a determined look that I'll never forget, and one that I always seek when I talk with new people. Some people say it's the "eye of the tiger." I say it's the look of desire.

John didn't have the money to run expensive newspaper or radio ads. He simply printed out hundreds of hot-pink flyers, inviting people to try his products and take a look at his opportunity. He then walked through the parking lots of Atlanta in the sun, in the rain, on the weekends and at night and handed them out one by one.

He wore an old blue suit and a pair of black shoes with holes in the bottoms. He walked up to hundreds of people and told them, "I'm getting rich and you can, too." John was like a rhinoceros charging across an asphalt jungle. He had guts. He was determined to be successful. Mostly, he got no's. Hundreds of them. Yet, he wouldn't give up. The thought of failure never entered his mind. The no's only made him work harder.

One morning, John charged into Chris Kauffman. Chris was upset. He'd just learned that he wasn't going to get an $18,000 commission check that he was counting on. He had been cut out of the deal.

"He was like a wild man," Chris recalls when he first spotted John. "He had an armful of pink flyers and he was getting ready to put one on my car."

"If you're looking to lose weight," John said, "I've got the perfect product for you. It even comes with a terrific opportunity."

"He was so excited I had to try his product," Chris recalled. "I bought one can of weight loss."

Chris didn't try the product right away. It was only through John's persistent follow-up that he finally agreed to make a shake while John listened in over the phone. Fortunately, Chris got great results and afterwards got into the business, too, and quickly proved that he was a born networker. Chris soon brought in Rick Moore, a super networker, and Rick brought in hundreds of people.

Today, John Quirk drives a new car, makes a six-figure income, and Sean has a diploma from the University of Michigan. In network marketing, anything can happen if you have enough desire, and an armful of hot-pink flyers.

I haven't handed out many flyers, because I don't have the kind of courage that John has. I also had a large center of influence. However, I have seen plenty of people use flyers and cards to build successful businesses. Flyers and cards come in two categories. One advertises the product and the other the opportunity. Of the two, the flyers and cards that promote the opportunity seem to work best. It can be as simple as this:

MAKE SERIOUS MONEY.

Is what you're doing right now going to pay you $4,000 per month working less than 40 hours per week? If not, call me 24 hours. (OOO) 555-1111.

Naturally, you would have to set up a phone mail system to handle all calls. You should record a friendly message that says something like, "Thanks so much for calling. If you'll leave your name and number, and the best time to get back with you, I'll set up an appointment so that we can discuss this exciting opportunity."

The fun thing about flyers is that you can post them in Laundromats, apartment complexes, school bulletin boards, phone booths and many other places.

Of course, if you have the courage to place them in people's hands, you'll be much more successful. You might think about saying something like this when you spot a potential customer or distributor: "Excuse me, but I'm introducing a new weight-loss product into our hometown market. If you know anybody who wants to lose weight, would you be so kind as to give them this flyer?"

Or, "Pardon me, but I've just started my own marketing company, and I'm looking for a few hard-working people who want to make some money. If you know anybody like that, would you mind passing this card along?"

Some people will ignore you, some will tell you to drop dead, some will take your card and never call, and once in awhile someone will show a real interest. Like everything else in the business, it's a numbers game. However, if you'll put a friendly smile on your face and excitement in your voice, you'll be amazed at what can happen.

Another way to generate customers and distributors is to run an ad in your local newspaper. Costs vary depending on the size of the newspaper, the length of the ad and the day of the week you run it. A Sunday ad in the "sales help wanted" section always worked best for me. In most papers you can figure four or five lines is going to cost between $100 and $300.

Make sure that you check with your company before you run any kind of ad, because some don't allow it. Others say it's OK so long as you don't use the company name. In the industry, we call that a blind ad. Mindy Jones once ran this blind ad in Atlanta:

"Do something great for your career, QUIT!"

Surprisingly, she got about 20 calls, which she quickly turned into a number of new customers and distributors.

When it comes to advertising, sometimes less is more. Running ads is not easy because you're going to deal with all sorts of people. Some of them, I'm afraid to say, won't be nice. Of course, you can screen your calls by leaving a friendly message on a voice-mail system. However, I think that a real person answering a phone is always more effective.

If you've never done it before, it takes guts. I've watched people spend hundreds of dollars on an ad, and then when the phone rings, they pray that's it's not someone calling about their ad. They're that terrified. Don't be. For the most part, the people calling are just like you. And remember, they're nervous, too. Besides, the person on the other end might be the one who makes you a very rich person. You never know.

The one thing that I do know from my experience and by watching dozens of distributors in action, is that once you do a few calls you get over your fear.

It should go something like this:

"Ring, ring."

"Hello, this is Tom."

"Yes, I was calling about your ad in the paper."

"Hey, thanks for calling. What's your name?"

"Bill Smith."

"Well, Bill, could you tell me a little about yourself?" (This question helps to put the caller at ease, and it also helps you to learn about them.)

"For the past 10 years I've been selling real estate, and I'm really looking to try something different."

"Well, Bill, I think I've got something here that you're probably going to be very interested in. I've got an appointment available at 9 a.m. tomorrow and another one at 2:30. Which one can you make?

Use the phone to set appointments. They can't see or taste your products or services over the phone. They can't see your compensation plan over the phone. You are simply trying to sell yourself and make an appointment. If they push for more information, stick to your guns.

"Bill, I really can't get into it right now because my other phone is ringing off the hook. Let's get together so you can see my product line and the compensation plan. Maybe it's not for you, and maybe it is. But we need to meet face to face. You said you wanted out of the real estate business. I think I've got the ticket. When can we get together?"

If the person insists on more information, you might consider giving them the company name and a little about your product line. Just try not to get into too much selling over the phone, because you aren't as powerful there as you are in person. The best way to learn solid phone skills is to watch someone in action who handles a lot of ad calls. Then do it.

Radio advertising is another tool that more and more distributors are using to generate leads these days. Again, depending on the market, the size of the station, and the length of the program, radio time can cost anywhere from a couple hundred dollars to several thousand dollars an hour. Some MLM companies have put together excellent information commercials that their distributors can use in either one hour or half-hour time slots.

One way to cut costs is to get several distributors to go in together and share expenses and leads. Call a number of stations in your market and find out if they do information commercials. Negotiate a contract, get the tapes from your company, and go to work.

Listeners will be given a number to call over the air. Again, you can use either voice mail, in which callers can leave their name and number, or you can take the calls live. I've used radio in the past in the St. Louis market. The response was only fair. I figured I paid about $55 a lead, and that's expensive.

Mindy Jones has done very well with radio ads in the Atlanta market. Joe and Carol Felger have also enjoyed quite a bit of success using radio programs in Chicago. As a rule, however, radio is costly and most distributors can't afford it.

There are other cold market tools as well. Working trade shows is one that comes up from time to time. I've tried that before, but I've never done very well with them, and I don't know of any distributors who have.

If it's a busy show, and you have a nice booth in a good location, you can talk to lots of folks. The problem is that most of the ones you follow-up with don't remember you or your products. They simply went to the show to get free goods. I discovered that the best prospects at a trade show were usually the people working the booths.

Direct-mail advertising is becoming more and more popular with networkers. One of the advantages of direct mail is that it lets you target a specific audience. There are many mailing lists that are available by firms that specialize in network marketing mailing lists. These are firms that have lists of potential networkers looking for the right business opportunity.

Although I haven't used it in my business yet, there are those who believe that the information highway, the Internet, will be the networkers next great tool. Here a networker can use their computer to talk to the world about their products and opportunity, and even create their own advertising page to attract prospects.

As you can see, there are many ways to generate leads for your business through the cold market, and I've only touched on a handful. I've seen distributors advertise on billboards, place home-made signs at busy intersections, take out ads in trade publications and magazines, and even hire their own children to pass out flyers and door hangers.

I once had a distributor in Atlanta that dressed up in a duck costume and walked around shopping centers passing out flyers and cards. He was very funny, but not very successful. It seemed that people didn't like buying stuff from a six-foot duck.

Chapter 16

Sponsoring Vs. Recruiting, There Is A Difference

"It seems to me shallow and arrogant for any man in these times to claim he is completely self-made, that he owes all his success to his own unaided efforts. Many hands and hearts and minds generally contribute to anyone's notable achievements."   — Walt Disney

The most important part to building a large distribution network is sponsoring. Whether we like to admit it or not, we are only as good as the people we bring into the business. I use the word sponsoring instead of recruiting because there is a big difference between the two designations.

Some networkers are master recruiters. They use ads and other cold-market tools to bring in the masses. Their philosophy is simple: throw 'em up against a wall and see who sticks. They crunch people the same way an accountant crunches numbers. They're only interested in the bottom line.

In the industry, there are successful distributors who have built large organizations using this technique. The problem is that they left a lot of dead bodies in their wake. And once a person has been burned in MLM, it makes it very difficult, if not impossible, to get him involved in the industry again. Tragically, some of these discarded people might have made successful networkers if someone had taken the time to train and support them.

Although sponsoring takes more work, it's the best way to do the business. Recruiters get people to sign on the dotted line, wish them luck, and then hustle off to sign up someone else. When you sponsor someone, you make a pledge to be there for them, to teach them what you know, to be their biggest cheerleader, and even their best friend.

A good sponsor learns what their new distributors want, and then goes to work to help them get it. You see, master networkers aren't concerned about what they want. Instead, they are driven by the needs of their people. Bob Montgomery taught me this lesson early in my career.

"If you'll help enough people to get what they want," Bob said, "you won't have to worry about what you want."

That's what sponsoring is all about. You're people engineering, and it takes all kinds of people to build your organization. As a leader, your job is to develop, teach and encourage your downline. Many will move small amounts of products, and a few will sell boatloads. You need both groups to succeed, and you need to appreciate your small distributors as much as your big ones.

Understand, too, that some folks will get excited about the opportunity for a week, some for a month, and some for a year. The successful distributors, however, will get excited and stay excited until they succeed. When you have a few of those in your organization, the business becomes easy.

At the time of this writing, I had 10 strong front lines, people committed to the long haul who aren't going anywhere else. A number make very good money. Of course, I didn't get them overnight, and I had to sponsor more than 50 to find those 10.

Keep in mind that good compensation plans have a thing called compression. That means if someone drops out in your line, the people below all move up. Some of my front lines are a result of compression, which allows the cream to rise to the top. As a result, the longer you're in the business, the stronger your lines become as the good people stay and the less-enthusiastic weed themselves out.

Early in my career, I used to become morose when people dropped out. I've since learned that attrition is as much a part of MLM as it is any other business. It doesn't matter what sort of profession you're in — real estate, banking, construction, teaching, journalism, baseball or insurance — some people will quit and some will stick it out and eventually succeed. So long as you've done all that you can to support and teach your people, you can't take it personally when they toss in the towel.

Looking back, I can see how even the ones no longer doing the business, helped me to continue. For a while, they were part of my organization, and for a time, they helped support me and others. Even so, I truly miss some of the folks who gave up on themselves and their dreams.

I want you to understand that I've had my share of ups and downs in the business. Just because I'm successful at this stage of my career doesn't mean that I didn't have plenty of no's and a flood of people who broke my heart. The choice that Karen and I had to make was to either keep on trying, or to join the ranks of the quitters.

I can laugh about it now, but in my first few months in multi-level marketing, I figured there were so many great folks in my organization that I was set for the rest of my life. One of them was a fellow that I'll call George. George came to me off an opportunity ad that ran in the sales section of the Orlando Sentinel. It went something like this:

RETIRE IN TWO YEARS

*If you want to make $8,000
a month and be your own boss
I'll show you how. Must be
willing to work hard and be
teachable. Call for an
appointment.*

George telephoned and made an appointment. When we got together, he became excited and purchased several cases of product, which is what I expect from a new distributor. After all, how can you distribute products or make money if you don't have anything to sell?

Because George had just moved to Central Florida, he knew very few people. So I ran ads for him in order to help build his organization. We did presentations all over town with the people that came from the ads, and the people that they knew. His organization took off like a wildfire and I just knew he was destined to become a master networker, who was going to help make me a fortune. Stupidly, I loaned George a couple thousand dollars worth of product.

When I finally got a check from him, it bounced higher than a super ball. As I drove to his apartment to confront him about the rubber check he had passed me, I had a huge knot in my stomach. My worst fears were realized. George was gone, and I never saw him again. To make matters worse, when George vanished, so did most of the people in his downline. And when they left, so did a bunch of others.

At that stage in my business, the loss nearly ended my MLM career. Karen was so angry about the bad check that she threatened to tie me to a cypress stump in the swamp behind our house and chum for alligators. To this day, I carry that check in my briefcase just to remind me about the difference between good business practices and starry-eyed stupidity.

Karen and I were in a tight spot and we knew it. There was only one way out, and I dreaded doing it. About a year earlier, when Karen's granddad passed away, he left us his 1977 Cadillac, a beauty with only 12,000 miles on the odometer. Unfortunately, it was as big as the Queen Mary and nearly as expensive to operate. Still, it was Karen's car, and because her granddad had willed it to her, she treasured it.

The night I approached her about selling it is one that I'll never forget. It was in the kitchen, and she was still angry with me for my stupidity. I couldn't blame her. She stood at the sink with her back to me shucking fresh corn.

"Honey," I said in my softest voice. "I have an idea that might get us out of this mess. If it's OK with you, maybe we could sell the Cadillac."

When she became very still, I swallowed hard, certain that I was again bungling everything. But then, after what seemed forever, she said in almost a whisper, "If that's what you have to do, go ahead and do it."

Starting to touch her back, I hestitated, knowing it was a gratuitous gesture. "I don't know of any other way," I said, my voice cracking. "We're out of product and money. I'm sorry I was so stupid, but I know I can do this thing. I know I can. I have to."

Slowly, she turned and faced me. Huge tears streamed down her cheeks. Her blue eyes were rimmed in red. "Of course, you can do it," she said through her tears. "You sell that dumb old car and go back to work."

Something happened to me in that instant. Before me stood the most important person in my life. I had let her down by being foolish with our money. Now, she was giving me her most prized possession.

At that moment, Karen was no doubt the only person in the world who believed that I could be successful in Reliv. She stood like a rock, and from her strength and love, I grew.

With the $1,200 we received for granddad's car, I bought products. Then, I went out with heart and boldness and sponsored one of my tennis buddies, two of my sisters, three close friends, Karen's brother, a neighbor, several people who came in off a newspaper ad, a couple of Karen's friends and one of her aunts.

I let everyone know that I was searching for leaders, people who weren't afraid to work and dream big, and people who weren't quitters.

"I'm not looking for great salespeople," I told them, "but I am looking for great people. Who do you know who is a self-starter and doesn't want to spend his or life watching *Bowling for Furniture* on television?"

When I got excited and strong, my new distributors got excited and strong, too. There was no doubt in our minds that we were going to build a company and a life together. No dream stealers were going to stop us.

I felt like Colonel Travis at the Alamo. I verbally took my sword out and drew a line in the sand.

"Who ever wants to make a commitment to doing this thing together for the rest of our lives, and never give up, step across this line," I said.

I was on a mission and nothing was going to stop me. There was no time to think about failure. When one of those negative snipers got in between my ears and started firing off rounds, I quickly flushed him out. One of Karen's friends had a friend in Atlanta.

I charged up there and met people like Mindy Jones and Michele Hembree, two women destined to become master networkers. It was in Atlanta, too, where I discovered my old buddy, Larry Garner, and his lovely wife, Linda.

Together, we made lists of all the people we knew, did hot-pink flyers, tacky newspaper ads and opportune moments. We brought in layers and layers of people. Everywhere we went, we took our products.

Once Mindy and I were in an elevator after we had done a presentation in an office building. We had an armful of goods.

"What do you have there," a fellow in the elevator asked, spying the cans in Mindy's arms.

"The best weight-loss product in the world," Mindy replied. "Want some?"

Not only did the stranger want some, but he took us up to his office where Mindy and I did another presentation and picked up a few more customers. We made it a habit to be visible with our products at Little League games, schools, work, our children's activities and everywhere else we went.

We wore shirts and buttons that advertised our products and opportunity. If we saw someone we liked, we invited them to an opportunity meeting. If we saw someone we didn't like, we invited them to an opportunity meeting, too. We learned that you never know who someone might know. We also learned that you never know who someone might blossom into.

Mindy sponsored one woman who I was sure had no business being in network marketing. She just didn't seem to have the personality for it. But this woman happened to know someone from Australia, and she asked if Mindy and I would talk with him and a few of his buddies.

Reluctantly, I agreed. Just before the meeting, I burned my hand while making a fire. Karen quickly bandaged me up — one of the benefits of being married to a nurse — and I drove over to Mindy's house. Mindy lived in a marvelous home. She had been successful before joining Reliv running her own marketing company and dress shop. The downside was that she worked so much that she had little time for her daughter, Sarah. Her Reliv business solved that problem.

John Hills, Ross Marshall and Brian Folbigg met with us in Mindy's living room. Bandaged hand and all, I gave the three Australians a presentation, outlining the financial opportunity on the back of an old wine poster that Mindy had pulled out of her garage.

"We want to do this thing," Brian said after I got finished. "We'll probably need about $700,000 worth of tins to get it going."

"Two questions," I gasped. "Did you say $700,000 and what the heck is a tin?"

As it turned out he did indeed say $700,000 and a tin was Australian for can. Mindy and I hit a homer that day, all because someone who I didn't think was a networker knew some fellows from Australia who were. After that, I never pre-judged anyone.

I was on a roll, thanks to the hard work of my downline, and before you could say "bad check," my organization took off like a snowball tumbling down a mountain side.

Chapter 17

Follow-up Can Make Your Fortune

"I do not fear failure. I only fear the slowing up of the engine inside of me, which is pounding, saying, 'Keep going, someone must be on top, why not you?'"

— George Patton, Jr.

S uccessful distributors do those things that others don't like doing. One of the basics is following up with customers. Learn to be tenacious in your follow-up and you will build a healthy retail base that will provide a constant source of leads. If you're lazy in this area, you'll find it difficult to build a loyal customer base.

Again, one of the major differences between buying a product off the shelf in a retail store, and buying a similar product from a networker, is that the networker comes with the goods. It's as if he or she jumps right out of the container of weight-loss, car cleaner, skin care, or whatever is being sold, and says to the customer, "I'm going to teach about my products and I'm going to make sure you like the results. If you don't, I'm going to give you your money back."

Master networkers make a commitment to their customers and provide them with superior service. They spoil them to a point where they would rather have a tooth drilled than buy from anyone else. They send their customers cards and personalized notes thanking them for their business. Like this one!

Dear Linda,

I can't begin to thank you enough for taking time out of your busy schedule to meet with me on Monday. Your home is lovely and your hospitality put me right at ease. I want to thank you, too, for trying my weight-loss products.

There is no doubt in my mind that you're going to lose those 30 pounds before your high school reunion this summer. You'll be the talk of the class. Not only that, but you'll have to buy a whole new wardrobe, and we know how much fun that can be.

I'll be calling this week to see how well you're doing, and to give you some encouragement if you need it. You can do it. Thanks again for your business.

Sincerely...

Notes and letters mean a lot to people. Unfortunately, most of us don't take the time to write them in our personal or business lives. Indeed, letter writing has become a dying art, which is a pretty sad commentary on our society.

Back in my Army days, nothing meant more to me than receiving a letter. Mail call was the highlight of the day, especially when there was a letter from home. It was the pits to come away empty-handed. Think about how good it makes you feel when you receive a thank-you note from someone showing their appreciation. That's the same experience you want your new customer to have.

In addition to the thank-you notes, you want to follow up with phone calls. Not chat sessions, but rather polite little conversations to make sure that your customer is using the products properly and getting favorable results. If there's a problem, you are there to work them through it.

Follow-up will come easier if you don't think of a customer as a one-time sell worth 10 bucks, but rather a lifetime of sells worth hundreds of dollars. Thinking of your customers that way will help you to place more value on them, and to better appreciate the importance of follow-up.

Besides, I've always found it easier to keep old customers happy than to gain new ones. Not only that, but if you do a good job with your customer base, each will become an excellent source for providing new customers and distributors.

Not long ago, I was doing follow-up calls with Jimmi Hooper, a Reliv distributor from South Carolina. Jimmi said she wanted me to talk with a fellow who wasn't having any success with our weight-loss program. As it turned out, the customer was taking his two shakes a day. However, late at night, he was into the refrigerator so often that he burned out two light bulbs.

"If you're serious about losing weight, you're going to have to quit cheating," I told him. "Take the Ding-Dongs out from underneath your pillow."

The point here is not to buy into other people's stories. You know your products or services are topnotch. If there is a problem, it's probably because the customer isn't taking them properly or just wasn't serious in the first place. If a customer becomes a problem, it's better to cheerfully refund them their money and go out and find a new customer. Some folks aren't going to be satisfied no matter how good your service or products are. They will erode your confidence and should be avoided if possible.

Following up with new distributors is just as important as with your customers. They need to know that you are serious about teaching them the business and are willing to help them. The first 24 hours are the most critical because that's when they're all fired up, and that's when a friend or family member, who isn't keen on MLM, is likely to come along and hose them down.

"If you think you're going to make any money in one of those pyramid deals, you're out of your mind," someone might say. "Why don't you get a real job?"

Those are words I heard time and again, but was carried through the down times with an upline that was always ready to provide me a boost.

Eddie Hawkins of Chicago was one of those who was always available to help. As a rule, Eddie didn't talk much. He'd just call and say with the enthusiasm of a man planning a three-story house, "Tom, this thing's going to be big."

"Man, that's great, Eddie," I'd reply.

"Did you hear me, Tom? This thing is going to be really big!"

"I heard you."

"I mean it, this thing is going to be big."

That's all Eddie ever prodded me with, but for some reason it worked. I'd get all excited because a big-time distributor in my upline took the time to call and tell me that Reliv was going to be "big." Sometimes simple is best.

Reliv distributor Joe Felger of Chicago likes to describe following up with a new distributor as being a lot like playing a tennis match.

"You hit the ball over to their side of the court and wait for them to return it," Joe says. "If they do, then you hit it back again."

In other words, if you tell your distributor to make a list of all the people he knows, and he does it, then he's hit the ball back. If he doesn't make the list, then you can't have a match. But if he hands you a list the next day, and says, "When can we meet with some of these people?" he's put the ball back in your court.

"Why don't you set up some appointments for tomorrow," you answer, sending a forehand to his side.

"Why don't we see some of them tonight," he answers with an overhead smash.

"Why don't we get in my car and do it right now," you say, volleying the ball into the corner for the point.

It's fun to play ball with someone who's not afraid to hit the ball back. On the other hand, it's impossible to get something going with someone who never returns the ball. You'll find that with some distributors, you'll want it more for them than they want it for themselves. Remember, it's not what they say that counts, but rather what they do. If your follow-up is good, it won't take long to separate the players from the talkers. Serious networkers knock the cover off the ball.

Chapter 18

Building A System

"Build for your team a feeling of oneness, of dependence upon one another and of strength to be derived by unity."
— Vince Lombardi

Y ou can't expect to sign up distributors and then have them go off and be successful on their own. That would make as much sense as a football coach recruiting a team and then asking them to report on game day. Distributors need a system that they can tie into in order to be successful.

There are many different types of systems in the MLM industry. Not everyone agrees on what works best. What I want to share is what worked for me.

Some people will tell you that opportunity meetings are a thing of the past because in this busy world of ours it's hard to get prospects to attend them. I disagree. Network marketing is at its best when people are face to face, and there's no better way to do that than at a meeting with dozens if not hundreds of excited people.

For those of you who have never attended a multi-level marketing meeting, it can be a lot of fun. They're usually at someone's home or at a hotel. Unless it's your misfortune to have a long-winded speaker, the presentation should last no more than 45 minutes.

Most of the MLM meetings begin with a distributor talking about the company and its products, followed by a second speaker who explains the compensation plan. In addition, a handful of distributors or customers will often share their personal experiences about the products or the opportunity. In the industry, we call these testimonials.

I believe that anyone can give an opportunity meeting with a little practice and a good set of slides. Most companies sell slide presentations with all the important points printed right on them. If you can read, you're in business. Not only that, but if you have a new distributor in another part of the country, where there are no meetings, all they have to do is order the slides, and bingo, they're in business, too. In MLM, simple is always better.

The key to these meetings are new people. If you attend them with guests, the meetings are terrific. If you attend them by yourself, they're not much fun, and worse, you're not building your business.

Establishing weekly Tuesday night meetings was my first step when I became a distributor. It was a painful one, too, because it meant giving up my tennis league, something that I had been doing for years and thoroughly enjoyed. To be successful in this business, however, you're going to have to make some sacrifices in the beginning. But that's OK, because once you have built a distribution network, you'll have plenty of time to do the things you enjoy.

So I put down my oversized graphite tennis racquet and scheduled my first opportunity meeting at the Holiday Inn in Altamonte Springs, Florida. It was a disaster. Sort of like losing a tennis match 6-0, 6-0, only worse. It started when I told Mike Williams that I was going to pack the place with at least 100 people.

"Don't stand too close to the door," I cautioned him when we arrived. "Don't want you to get trampled by the crowd."

You can imagine my embarrassment when only eight people showed up, and two of those I grabbed in the hotel lobby out of desperation. I was so upset that I didn't want to do the presentation. Mike made me. Although it was a pitiful start in my MLM career, it did motivate me to get more people to the next meeting. When you spend $125 for a room, it only makes sense to fill it, and to get other people involved to share the expenses. Once you establish a core group of, say, a dozen people, then you can form a co-op and begin delegating responsibilities and collecting dues to cover expenses.

There are a number of things that must be done if your presentations are going to go smoothly. For a moment, think of yourself as a guest walking into a hotel in search of a meeting that a friend has invited you to. As you enter the hotel, you immediately spot signs directing you to the proper location.

Next, as you near the room, you spot two friendly people at a sign-in table stationed outside the room. They give you a warm greeting, give you a ''guest'' name tag to wear, and then help locate your friend. Once inside the room, you immediately notice that the air is filled with pleasant music and that the people are well-dressed and friendly.

To the front you spot an attractive product display, and a colorful assortment of company literature. A number of people come up and introduce themselves to you, and one even offers to get you a drink of water. As your friend escorts you to a seat, you think to yourself, ''I like being around these people.''

Master networkers understand that first impressions are critical. They go out of their way to make people feel at home, and they understand that guests are the lifeblood of their business. Nothing bugs me more than to watch a bunch of distributors chatting together in a corner while only a few feet away a new person stands alone. If you go out of your way to make other distributors' guests feel at ease, you can bet they will do the same for you. Remember, you are building a team, and players on successful teams support one another.

Another point to remember is to always put up fewer chairs than you think you will need. Nothing looks worse than a roomful of empty seats. On the other hand, when you're scampering around to add more chairs, it creates a sense of excitement.

Presentations must be simple so that anyone can do them. Professional speakers are great for corporate America, but in network marketing it's more important to let everyone participate. It promotes personal growth, and believe it or not, it's more powerful.

Not long ago, I witnessed one of the worst meetings that I have ever seen, and believe me, I've seen some dillies. This poor fellow couldn't even read the slides, and he was so nervous he could hardly breathe let alone talk.

A guest sitting next to me leaned over and said "This is the most pitiful presentation I've ever seen."

"Yeah, isn't it great," I said. "Just think, that guy's making about $4,000 a month. Imagine what you could do?"

The fellow smiled and sat back in his chair. After the meeting, he signed up and bought several cases of product.

"If a guy who can barely read can make money doing this, I know I can," he said.

The natural tendency is to put the most polished orators on the stage. There are a number of problems with this practice. One, it doesn't give the other folks a chance to grow, and two, it can intimidate your guests. Instead of your prospect thinking that "anybody can do this business," they're thinking, "I can see how that woman is making money. She's good, but I could never do that."

This may be hard for you to believe, but it took me more than six years to get Karen to do her first opportunity meeting. The only reason she did it then was so that she could get a friend, Donna Baker, to do it with her. You see, Donna was scared to death to talk in front of people.

The entire presentation lasted less than 15 minutes. It was the shortest meeting I have ever seen. It was so quick, in fact, that I thought about going to the hotel manager and seeing if I could get a refund. The funny thing is that everyone loved it. The guests hung around, no doubt a little surprised at the quickness of the meeting, and most of them signed on as distributors.

Today, Donna Baker travels throughout the Midwest giving meetings and teaching other people how to do the same. You see, if someone can gather the courage to get up and talk in front of a roomful of people, it makes it that much easier for them to go up and talk to anyone about their products or opportunity.

The most important part of the meeting are the testimonials. However, if the stories are to be effective, they need to be short and to the point. Sixty seconds is plenty of time to tell people that you've gotten great results on the products and that you'll never be without them. It's more than enough time to tell everyone that you're having a ball in the business, that you're making money, that anyone can do it and that you're getting help.

When I first moved to Atlanta, we had about 20 people at our meetings. I told the distributors that if we didn't raise that number to at least 50 by the following week, that I was going to walk to the front of the room, pour gasoline on myself, and light a match. Everyone laughed but me. Fortunately, we had 56 people at the next presentation.

The point is that all you have to do to build your meetings and, thus, your business, is for everyone to bring a new person each week. If you'll make a commitment to do that, you'll be more successful than your wildest dreams. And no excuses, because you have seven days to find one person. If necessary, tie them up and toss them into the back of your car. Do whatever it takes. Just bring new people.

Weekly trainings are also critical to your system, but I'm not going into that now because the next chapter is dedicated to that subject. However, there are a number of other important parts to your system. Let's take a look at some of them.

Conference calls are now being used by more and more MLM companies. The advantage of conference calling is that your prospect can listen in without leaving home. Reliv conference calls take place twice a week and involve thousands of people. For the most part, they are like the Tuesday night meeting, only you are listening to the speakers over the phone.

The home party plan is another way to present your products and opportunity. Some MLM companies were built around this simple concept. In Reliv, we call them shake parties and they are designed to get people on the weight-loss or nutritional programs.

All you have to do is invite some friends and neighbors over to your home. Make sure you tell them what you're up to because, as a rule, people aren't wild about surprises.

In Reliv, we make up all kinds of tasty shakes, pass around nutritional bars and sports drinks and, in general, have a good time. These events are less formal than ones held at hotels. There are plenty of folks who prefer this type of presentation, and oodles of them who have made a fortune doing it and teaching others how to do the same.

Another tool that I used to build my business I call the "beehive." That's when a half dozen or so distributors and I meet at someone's house. We tell our downlines in advance, so that they can bring guests. We usually do three presentations — one at 9 a.m., one at noon, and one at 3 p.m. They are similar to the hotel meeting, but like the home-party plan, less formal. Instead of a slide presentation, I like using a white board to show the marketing plan.

There are a number of advantages to using a beehive. One, you're in someone's home, so you can readily use the kitchen to prepare products, which is a great help if you're in the nutritional foods business like I am.

Living rooms are cheaper than hotel rooms and sometimes it's easier to get someone to drop by a home than to walk into a hotel. By offering different meeting times, it makes it easier for guests to attend, and when you're not doing presentations, you can use the time to call prospects or do a little training on the white board with your new people.

There is no better way to train new distributors on how to do presentations, handle objections, or talk on the phone than at beehives. I've also found that people have more courage when they're in a group. In other words, they're more likely to make calls when they see and hear others doing it than if they were at home by themselves.

When it comes to the phone, today's networkers are experts with three-way calling and speaker phones. While I still lived Orlando, I used a speaker phone to do training and meetings with my new group in Atlanta. They simply invited people to their homes, turned on the speaker phone, and I started blabbing away.

Three-way calling is another tool that today's networkers use to bolster their systems. This tool allows seasoned veterans to get on calls with their downline and help them to pitch the business and products to prospects as well as doing follow-up calls. Again, the rookie can borrow upline strength and learn at the same time.

Master networkers Joe and Carol Felger of Chicago, and Phil and Betty Wolf of Grand Rapids, Michigan, are all pros at three-way calling.

The last thing I want to mention is impending events. It's fairly common for companies to send officers and top distributors into the field for special meetings. Whenever this happens, make sure you promote it. Indeed, master networkers are master promoters, and they understand that the promotion of the event is more important than the event itself.

Of course, the biggest happening of the year for most MLM companies is the national conference. This is truly the place where you can meet the company big shots and the super-star networkers. Never miss a conference, and always take as many new people to them as possible. Besides being fun, you can learn a great deal about the company and other distributors at conferences. And if you're teachable and not afraid of work, it won't be long before you're up on stage telling everyone how you did it.

Master networkers use most if not all of the tools that I've shown you to create their systems. They understand the importance of generating massive action, and by teaching people how to do all of these things, you can bet that your organization is going to grow.

Earlier, I talked about the need to establish a healthy business for yourself. That means getting a base of retail and wholesale customers. The following step was to teach others to do the same, which allows you to earn commissions off of their efforts. The next move in that evolution is to teach people how to create systems in surrounding communities, states and even countries. If you learn how to do that, you'll be writing your own MLM book one day.

Chapter 19

Training Is All About Duplication

"A child miseducated is a child lost." — John F. Kennedy

I f you think my first opportunity meeting was a bust, wait until you hear what happened when I did my first training. Talk about an embarrassing moment.

In my first month in the business, Mike Williams did all of the training's. He had to, because he was the only one who knew what he was doing. Mike, however, realized that sooner or later that he was going to have to push me up and let me take a shot at a two-hour Saturday morning session. Like opportunity meetings, training's need to be held regularly.

To make matters worse, I was going to have to do my first class in front of the company's trainer. I was so nervous that I went to a great deal of trouble to prepare a detailed program with all sorts of professional sales techniques that I had gotten out of a stack of books at the Orlando Public Library. By golly, if he wanted to witness a training, I was going to give him a dandy. I had props, quotes, skits, and even a quiz for good measure.

Halfway through the program, the company trainer pulled me aside and asked me why I wasn't using the Reliv training outline.

"We've already done that a number of times," I answered. "I thought it was time for something new."

Tact was not this person's strong suit. He proceeded to lambaste me in a way that would have made an Army drill sergeant proud.

By the time he was finished, I felt about as tall as a toad but not nearly as important.

"What you're doing is not duplicable," he said. "You've got to stick to the basics, and you've got to keep it simple if you expect to build an organization."

"I'm not sure I know what you mean," I said. "Don't you think it's going to get a little boring if I do the same thing every Saturday morning?"

"Listen, anybody can teach a jackass to roll over," he said. "But when you can teach a jackass to teach a jackass to roll over, then you're onto something."

I wasn't sure that I liked the implication, but I certainly got the point. From that moment on, I stuck to the basics, followed the company outline and kept it simple. It worked, and because the training's weren't difficult to imitate, it wasn't long before I had trained other trainers, who were doing training's not only in Orlando, but in other parts of the country as well.

The lesson I learned was this: To be successful in MLM you must be duplicable, and to do that you must keep things simple. Since that day, I have done hundreds of training's all over the world, and have seen hundreds of more. Surprisingly, I have never been bored, and I have always learned something new, often from rookie distributors.

Like opportunity meetings, training's are geared for new people, and if you have a few first-timers sitting around you, I guarantee that you're going to have a good time. Networking is a fun, simple business that requires you to enjoy your products and share them with others. It does not, however, require you to know everything about your products. If you try to become an expert regarding the formulations and ingredients of nutrition, jewelry, car wax or whatever you sell, and then teach that to your downline, you're complicating the process. In network marketing, we sell results, and we do that by telling stories.

"Hey, Pam, you need to try this weight-loss I've been using. It's great."

"What's in it?" Pam asks.

"Heck, I don't know. All I know is that I lost 20 pounds in a month, and I feel great."

Now, if I start going into all the ingredients and explaining how they work, I've got problems. The process is now complicated and not duplicable. Instead of teaching people to go out and share their results, which anyone can do, now we've got to make nutritional experts out of them, and that will take years.

Here's another way to look at it. Suppose you go into a clothing store and pick up a dress off the rack. The salesperson comes over and immediately starts telling you that the fabric is a special Jamaican blend that comes from left-footed sheep, that the stitching is an underhand double-loop performed by girls no older than 15, and that the colors are preserved by double dipping them in a titanium pool.

None of that made any sense to you, and it shouldn't because it doesn't make any sense to me either. About that time another woman comes by and sees you eyeing the dress.

"I bought that very same dress a year ago and it's the finest outfit I've ever owned," she says. "Never in my life have I gotten so many compliments on a dress, and you know, it looks better now than the day I bought it."

One woman talked ingredients and one talked results. Which one is likely to get you to buy the dress? Which one is the more duplicable?

I'm not advocating that you shouldn't know anything about your product line, because you should. Certainly a basic understanding about how to use your products or services and why they're important for you is essential. Just be careful that you don't become "Mr. Know-It-All" and expect your people to do the same.

Perhaps the best way to deal with this issue is to let the company experts teach the technical stuff. Dr. Carl Hastings, a food scientist with a Ph.D. from the University of Illinois, does that for Reliv. It makes us feel good to hear him talk about ingredients and formulas and why certain products have been put together the way they have.

We have confidence in his abilities as well as the abilities of the other scientists and doctors who help him. At the same time, we know that our job is not to be a food scientist, but rather to go out and share the results of their work. It's a simple relationship. The scientists make the stuff and we sell it because we know it works. If you want to know more about what makes it work, talk to one of the scientists the first chance you get.

The first step in training a new distributor is to sit down with her and go through the distributor manual and highlight all the important information. Teach new people how to fill out order forms and distributor applications. Work closely with them until they understand how the marketing plan works, and can present it on the back of a napkin.

Make sure they know all the important numbers, such as the conference calls, and that they know where and when meetings and training's will be held. Impress on the new person the importance of using the system and never missing a meeting. Find out what their goals are let them know yours.

Those first one-on-one training's are critical, and so are your group training's. To be effective, they must be enjoyable, and to be enjoyable, they must have participation. When you get a whole roomful of people taking part in a class and sharing their ideas everyone feels a part and has a good time.

All good MLM companies have training outlines and programs. Don't try to re-invent the wheel. Use what's available, because a lot of time, thought, research and experience has gone into developing those outlines and programs. Fill your training with lots of stories and encourage others in the room to share theirs. I always start my meetings by asking, "Who has a good story to share this morning?" You'd be surprised at what people come up with. Sometimes they're funny, most of the times they're helpful, and all the time, they allow people to relax and feel like they're a part of the group.

Training's are also a great place to recognize people who have graduated to higher levels, to applaud their efforts and to show appreciation for their hard work. St. Louis Reliv distributors

Donna Baker and Mary Bachinski did a training recently that was nothing short of a hoot.

They told everyone how they had gone out after a meeting and talked to managers in convenience stores who worked the night shift.

"If you don't like the hours and the money you're making now, we can show you a better way," they said. "We'll show you how you can be home with your families at night."

A few days later, Donna and Mary had a roomful of convenience store people looking for a better way. It's my opinion that no one can do a better training than a new distributor who is on fire and having success. They put the fear of loss in everyone as they simply tell people how they are doing the business.

Another thing that I like to do in training's is to ask people what kind of objections they've heard during the week. When you think about it, we all hear the same ones time and time again. Once the list is posted on a white board, I like to go around the room and have volunteers tell the others what they say when someone says, "These products too expensive?" Or, "Is this MLM?" Or, "Am I going to have to sell?" Or, "I don't have any money."

When you use different trainers, and encourage distributor participation, no two meetings are ever the same. I learned the importance of sticking to the basics early in my MLM career and it has paid off in a big way. If I had insisted on doing it my way and making myself the issue, I would no doubt still be back in Orlando working with a handful of people. Instead, I have trainers all over the world sticking to the basics and teaching others to do the same.

I told you my worst training; now, I'm going to tell you about one of my favorites. It was in the summer of 1991, about 18 months after that terrible night in which I had wrecked my old van coming home from the Orlando Sentinel. I had just finished listening to master networker Michele Hembree from Atlanta conduct a two-hour class that almost had me jumping out of my chair with delight. She was real, she was enthusiastic, and she kept to the outline. Not only that, but there were more than 250 distributors in the room who were equally excited.

I was still buzzing when I pulled into my driveway, but nothing compared to the buzzing I'd be doing in a few minutes. When the garage door went up, my chin fell down to my knees. Right in front of me was a red Mercedes convertible and my beautiful bride.

"It's for you," she said. "New tires and all."

Chapter 20

Have Passion For Your Business

*"Satisfaction lies in effort, not in the attainment. Full effort
is full victory."*   — Mahatma Gandhi

A few years ago Karen and I flew out to California where we
met with former anti-war radical Jerry Rubin, who, in the
1960s, had founded the Youth International Party (Yip-
pies). Karen and I were on our way to Australia and New Zealand,
but we stopped off long enough to celebrate Jerry's birthday, and
meet with long-time MLM authority, Clifton Jolley.

At the time, I was the top distributor for Reliv and Jerry was the
star of Omnitrition, earning more than $600,000 in 1992. In the
1960s, Jerry had gone on trial with the Chicago Seven for his
participation in the anti-war riots at the Democratic National Convention. He was convicted but never served time in prison because
the U.S. Court of Appeals ruled that Judge Julius Hoffman had
made errors during the trial.

As a youth, he had made the statement, "Never trust anyone
over 30." In 1988, when he celebrated his 50th birthday and had
become one of the most successful network marketers in the country, he revised his statement to "Never trust anyone under 50."

Before he was tragically struck by a car while jaywalking and
killed in November, 1994, Jerry showed the same kind of revo-
lutionary passion for MLM that he once did for the Yippie anti-
war movement. So by the time he and I met on a warm California

night in 1991, the son of a union organizer who became a master of political theater and then a network marketing whiz and the son of a fireman who became paratrooper and then a network marketing advocate found peace with each other. The passions of the '60s, which had put us at opposite poles then, were replaced by the more positive passions of the '90s that made us brothers in MLM.

In a way, we were on the same team, in love with a new kind of revolution. We found it strange, yet comforting, so we said good-bye to the past, and toasted the entrepreneurial revolution of the future.

"The baby boomers are still searching for freedom," he said. "Only now, they're finding it in MLM."

Like so many other successful network marketers, Jerry was on a mission to help people to a better way of life. His passion was contagious, and his love for MLM was greater than the dislike he once had for the so-called Establishment. People followed him by the hundreds as he embraced his MLM freedom crusade because he loved what he was doing.

Mary Kay Ash understood the power of a worthwhile crusade. She was unhappy with the way men sometimes treated her in the workplace and knew there must be thousands of other women who felt the same way. As a result, she vowed to provide women with an opportunity that allowed them to earn good money while working out of their homes. Freedom was the battle cry, and freedom allowed her beauty consultants to set their own hours so that they could be home when they needed to be, and at work when they wanted to be.

To truly be successful in MLM, you have to love what you are doing with all your heart, and get other people to love it. Jerry Rubin understood the power of passion, so did Mary Kay Ash, and so does Bob Montgomery. Bob's vision was to create a company that would provide healthy foods and drinks to an unhealthy nation.

He knew that food was the No. 1 industry in America. He also realized that the No. 2 industry was health care, or perhaps sick care would be a better term. It was obvious to him that the two were connected. Today, Bob and Sandy Montgomery, along with thousands of Reliv distributors, are on a mission to get people to eat better, to exercise and, in general, to take better care of themselves.

The beauty of MLM is that the mission can become a two-pronged attack. On one hand, you have your product line and all that it can do for people, and on the other, you have the opportunity and all that it can provide for people. Indeed, providing additional income for struggling families is a cause that gets my juices flowing.

With American workers getting laid off by the thousands, and with the rising costs of college, housing and retirement, the future can create some scary images. Saving accounts are dwindling and the cost of living is soaring. What's a person to do?

Why, MLM of course. It simply allows a person to create a distribution network that can generate residual income to help build retirement or college funds, or pay your bills. If you construct your part of it large enough, and with the right company, it can furnish enough income to take care of you for the rest of your life, and then you can will your business to your children. Providing for the future of my family is something that I am passionate about.

What troubles me is that people express their worries about how they're going to pay their bills or provide for their retirement, but do nothing about it. They think about doing MLM, but they are afraid to extricate themselves from the couch and make a few calls. I'll tell you what scares me to death, that's wasting my life sitting in front of the TV.

I always ask my new distributors to tell me what their passions in life are. In other words, what do they really love to do, or what do they really want to do with their lives. It's sad, but many people are so caught up in the day-to-day routine of surviving, that they've totally lost sight of their dreams.

Take the time to rediscover those dreams. I've yet to hear of anyone on their deathbed say if they could do it over again, they would spend more time at the office. Instead, they talk about spending more time with their families and being a better mother, father, wife or husband.

My passion in life is God and family. I want to follow the tenets that God seems to have constructed into my conscience and, if I work at it, it stands to reason that I will become the kind of family man I want to be. Not only do I want to be the best husband in the world for Karen, but a loving and caring father for our children. I want to write books that can guide people to a more productive lifestyle, and to help them to better health and wealth. These are the passions that fuel my fire.

Once I realized that Reliv was the vehicle that would allow me to pursue these passions, I had no problem getting off the couch, turning off the television and going out into the world and talking my head off. Look around and you'll notice that the truly successful people live life with passion. They love what they do and it shows. Not only that, but their gusto for life and their positive attitude is so attractive that people want to be around them.

Remember, people are watching you as you begin your journey into MLM, and if they see that you love it and are passionate about it, they'll want to know more. On the other hand, if they see you plodding along with a weary scowl on your face, they'll make up every excuse in the world not to meet with you.

It's important to love what you do in life and to be passionate about it. If you don't have that now, find it. Life is too short to be miserable, and you'll certainly never make it in network marketing with a frown on your face.

Chapter 21

Treat Your Business Like A Business

"Far and away the best prize that life offers is the chance to work hard at work worth doing."   — Theodore Roosevelt

Most of the people who get involved with an MLM company have never been in business for themselves before. They're used to working for someone else and collecting a check at the end of the week. That's not the way it works when you're an independent contractor.

In most cases, the MLM company you work for is going to send you a commission check at the end of the month, and since you're not an employee, they're not going to withhold state or federal income taxes. As an independent contractor, it will be up to you to pay your own income taxes, and you'll need to do that on a quarterly basis.

On more than one occasion, I've seen distributors spend everything they make without putting money aside to pay their taxes. That's a mistake. As soon as you start making money, get with an accountant. He'll tell you how much money you'll need to pay Uncle Sam each quarter and what kind of records you'll need to keep.

Now, before you start squawking about keeping a record or two, keep in mind that all business owners have to do the same thing. Hey, it's the price you pay for being the CEO of your own company. The good news is that you don't have any employees to keep track of, and most MLM companies do the lion's share of the record-keeping for you.

Profits are especially easy to keep track of if your company handles orders from both your retail customers and your distributors. If that's the case, teach them to order directly from the company. That way the company keeps track of your profits and sends you a check at the end of the month. Another nice thing about this system is that you don't have to warehouse or handle goods. Pretty simple, isn't it?

Every 90 days you simply add up the checks that you received from the company, deduct your business expenses, and what you have left is your profit. At that point, set aside some for Uncle Sam. Of course, if you're selling directly to customers and wholesalers, you'll need to keep track of those profits and include them as well.

Keep in mind that there are a lot of advantages to owning your own business, especially if you work out of your house. For example, you can deduct a percentage of most home expenses if you have an office in your house. Make sure to keep accurate mileage records when you use your car for business. Keep track, too, of advertising expenses, office supplies and equipment, hotel room costs, phone bills and money you spend taking prospects out to lunch or dinner.

It's best if you set up an office in your house and put a file cabinet in it for record keeping. I have folders for orders, invoices, customers, distributors, training and expenses. I also have a separate checking account and credit card just for my business, which also helps me to keep track of my expenses.

The most important piece of equipment in your office is your telephone. Make sure you get one that you like. It doesn't matter if it's a Snoopy phone or one shaped liked a tennis shoe. If you like it, that's all that counts. Phones are your lifeline in this business, so make sure it's in a quiet spot where you can make follow-up calls to your customers and distributors without too many interruptions.

If the phone you now have doesn't have a speaker mode, make sure you get one. They come in handy when you have people over and you want to listen to a conference call. Also invest the extra few bucks a month to get call waiting and three-way calling. Master networkers spend a lot of time on the phone, and they know how to use them.

A distributor came up to me not long ago and said she was going to quit the business because she wasn't making any money. I was a bit surprised because I knew that she had a dozen or so customers and even a couple of distributors in her downline.

"How much product did you sell last month?" I asked her.

"Around $1,100 worth," she answered. "Maybe a little more."

She was buying her product at a 45-percent discount, and I knew that most of those sales were at retail, which meant that she had to have made $400 or $500. The problem was that as soon as she made a sale, she spent the money on other things. She had no idea where the money was going because she wasn't keeping track of her profits, and in a sense was stealing from her own business. Don't make the mistake of squandering your money. Treat your business like a business or you won't have one for long.

When you work full-time for someone else, you put in at least 40 hours per week. You arrive at work on time, you come back from lunch on time and you quit on time. If you don't, you get fired.

When you're in business for yourself, you don't have anyone looking over your shoulder. You're on your own to work when you want and to play when you want. This can be both good and bad, depending on the kind of person you are. If you're a self-starter, you'll relish your freedom, but at the same time work harder for yourself than you ever did for anyone else. If you're a bit on the lazy side and need a swift kick to get going, you're going to have to change your ways.

In MLM, there are no bosses. Everyone is an independent contract or responsible for their own business. If you're working full-time, make sure you put in the same amount of hours for yourself that you used to when you worked like a dog to make someone else rich.

Working, by the way, is not getting on the phone and chit-chatting with other distributors about something the company did or didn't do or about what Ted said about Alice. There will always be professional time-killers who want to gossip and waste your day. My advice to you is to stay away from them.

To me, work in this business is only one thing — talking to new people about your products and opportunity. Anything else is just an excuse to keep from doing what you should be doing. With that in mind, I've yet to meet a networker who has ever put in a 40-hour work week. If someone did, they'd make a fortune.

Chapter 22

The Ugly Side Of MLM

"If you work hard on building your business and improving yourself, you'll have little time to criticize others."   — TP

I can't begin to count the times that I've heard people say after hearing an MLM presentation that "it sounds almost too good to be true." Well, for the most part the industry is as good as networkers want you to believe it is, but I'd be misleading you if I didn't point out a few of the pitfalls.

MLM is certainly not immune to having its share of rogue companies and rascal distributors. Of course, the same can be said about insurance, banking, politics, real estate, law or any other profession. All of them have their scoundrels. The trick, of course, is to identify honest people and companies and stay away from the others.

One of the ghastly things that can happen to a new networker is to get involved in an MLM company, get a lot of their friends to follow them, and then have it go down the drain like dirty bath water. When that happens, not only do they feel sick, but even worse, they feel terrible for the folks that they brought in. The best way to keep such a thing from happening is to do your homework on a corporation before jumping on board.

Unfortunately, even when you are in a good company that is geared for the long haul, there will be plenty of people who will give up and quit. Most of them won't be honest enough to admit that it was their fault. They won't own up to the fact that they didn't work, go to training's or meetings. They'll simply blame you, the products or the company for their failure.

Sometimes these people are destined to fail from the beginning. That's because the person who signed them up promised that they would get rich without having to work. The only way that could happen is if you got lucky and sponsored a super networker on your first try, and the chances of doing that are slim.

Front-end loading is another activity that has given the industry a black eye in the past. This is an ugly practice of selling new distributors more products than they need. It's OK for a hard-working newcomer to buy a bunch of product in order to get a better discount. They understand that they can make more money selling products at a 45% discount than a 25% discount.

It's another thing to sell $5,000 worth of goods to a 90-year-old grandmother who lives in a small town and doesn't know anybody. If you sell a trunkful of products to a new distributor, you'd better plan on helping them to move it. If you don't, you're probably guilty of front-end loading, and that's a nasty practice that will catch up to you sooner or later.

Another thing to be leery of is ridiculous income claims. Sometimes people get so caught up in the excitement of the business that they start telling all kinds of financial whoppers. And just as bad are the people in your downline who will often puff up your income story. In most walks of life, folks don't go around bragging about how much money they make, but in MLM it seems to be part of the business.

"My goal is to make as much money as people say I do," Reliv distributor Tom Moody told me not long ago. "If I tell people I'm making $30,000 a month, by the end of the day they're telling everyone I'm making $50,000 a month."

The reality is that not everyone is going to get rich in MLM, but plenty of folks can supplement their incomes. Many others can generate healthy earnings while enjoying the rewards and freedom of owning their own business. Honesty is always the best policy, or like Abraham Lincoln said, "No man has a good enough memory to make a successful liar."

Similar to the income boasts, some networkers make outrageous product claims in an attempt to get folks to try their goods. They sound something like this:

"Take a sip of this stuff and you'll lose 50 pounds by Friday and you'll never have cancer. If you take two sips, you'll really get great results."

I don't care if you're selling make-up, jewelry, car wax, perfume or vitamins, you don't need to make outlandish claims. Most network-marketing companies have excellent products that customers will enjoy without overselling them. Besides, when you exaggerate their quality to the point of nonsense, you're setting your customer up for disappointment.

Another thing that drives me nuts is watching people on stage one night talking about how great their company's products are, how wonderful the people are, and how they'll never do anything else. Then they quit the next day and join another MLM company. To make matters worse, they start trying to recruit your downline into their new company. People who do that are lower than foot fungus. Though I've witnessed the routine a number of times, I've yet to see one of those characters become successful.

I sponsored a fellow once who was desperate to make money. He was truly a decent person or, at least, I thought he was, and I made a commitment to work right along with him. Karen and I opened our home to him and his people for meetings, training's and shake parties. In less than 12 weeks, he was earning more than $2,000 a month, and was on his way.

Then the ugly thing happened. Someone came along and told him that he could make more money by joining their company. He bought into a bunch of junk without even talking to me. Some of his new distributors followed him, some stayed and some got confused and quit. A few weeks later, he realized he had made a mistake, and a few months later, his new company went down the tubes.

I ran into him not long ago.

"I never should have left," he said. "I did a stupid thing. Do you think we could start over?"

"I'm afraid not," I told him. "You didn't appreciate what you had and what people did for you. The trust is gone."

He went away sad and so did I. He was so close to reaching his dreams. When so-called friends jump ship, it's a slap in the face and ugly to the bone. But it happens, and when it does, the best thing to do is turn the page.

After you've been in the business for a while, you'll notice that the negative people like to hang out together and bad-mouth everything and everybody. My advice is to not let them drag you into their whiny conversations. If you do, they'll suck the dreams right out of your head.

When I first got into MLM, I let the complainers waste a lot of my time. Not now. I don't want people calling me up at all hours of the day to moan about this and that. Once they learn that you're not going to listen to them, they quit calling and find some other sucker to kill time with.

I've often said that the best thing about MLM is the people, and the worst thing about MLM is the people. To be successful in this business of people engineering, you need to build it with positive folks and let the negative ones weed themselves out.

Ironically, unsuccessful folks aren't necessarily the only ones who fail. Heck, I've seen successful distributors who have made it to the top suddenly start complaining and whining about the company, other distributors and the color of their Mercedes. I guess they forgot where they came from.

Sadly, I've seen them do it to the point where they run themselves right out of the business. I suppose some folks aren't satisfied unless they're unhappy and complaining to everyone around them. People like that remind me of the fellow who became a monk. As the story goes, he joined a monastery that allowed the monks to speak only two words a year.

At the end of the first year, the new monk was called into the office where the head monk allowed him to speak his two words.

"Food's bad," the new monk said.

A year went by, and the monk was again called into the office to speak.

"Bed's hard," he said.

After another year passed, he was again asked to speak.

"I quit," answered the monk.

"Well, it's no wonder," answered the head monk. "You've done nothing but complain since you've been here."

In every walk of life there are the downers that drain a person, or want to make you walk away from something that is basically terrific. Recognize the downers even if you can't ignore them, then keep them at arm's length. Think of it as going over a bad road. Once you've made that trip, you steer around it the next time.

Chapter 23

Keep Egos Out Of The Business

"There is no experience better for the heart than reaching down and lifting people up."   — John Andrew Holmer

The most frustrating part of this business for me is dealing with individuals who can't get it through their titanium-coated heads to boost their people instead of themselves. This is perhaps the most important secret to becoming successful in this industry, and perhaps in life itself. We live in the "me-first age" and to prosper in MLM, you need to be in the "you-first age."

I've watched in horror as distributors got jealous of people in their own downlines and started fighting with them. Now I ask, does it make sense to fight with people who are making money for you?

Nothing is so unattractive as a group of people who have bad feelings toward one another. New people to the business can spot the tension a mile away, and it's not an environment that they want to become a part of. On the other hand, a room filled with distributors who get along, and who are working hard to help one another, is as inviting as a Florida spring on a hot summer day.

It's ridiculous to fight over such silly things as who is going to do a meeting or a training. Much more can be accomplished if you learn to work out your differences in a calm and respectful way. If you battle with one another, you'll never reach your goals.

Everyone will be so busy worrying and gossiping about who said what to whom that no one will do any work.

There's no way I could keep track of all the times that people have done cruel things to me. I'd be a liar if I said it didn't hurt. However, I have learned that it doesn't do any good to strike back in anger. If your goal is to build a distribution network with all kinds of people, you must handle hurtful incidents with kindness and forgiveness.

Early in our careers, Karen and I made a pact never to say bad things about people in our organization to anybody no matter what someone had said or done. It's amazing how quickly fires go out when you smother them with silence. If you're really mad at someone, never pick up the phone and call them while your heart is racing. Don't write them a letter or rush over to their house either. Wait a few days, and you'll be surprised at how much better you'll handle the situation.

I've watched in disbelief as people who were once nothing, suddenly become stars in the industry and turn into megalomaniacs. Their heads get so big they can't fit into convention centers. They start believing all the nice things that people say about them.

To make matters worse, they become such big shots that they want to run the company and everybody else. They forget about network marketing and get into corporate politics. Hey, if you're ahead, stay quiet and enjoy it.

Mary Kay Ash teaches her beauty consultants to treat people the same way that they would like to be treated. It's such a simple little golden rule that it's often overlooked. The fact is that to be a master networker you need to get along with everyone. That means your upline, sideline, the company and especially your downline.

If you put your people first and always give them the credit for your success, they'll take you to the moon in a stretch limo. If you fight with them, take all the credit and get jealous when they succeed, they'll want to drag you off the stage and dip you in hot chocolate. Be passionate but humble. Never forget where you came from, and remember, you are only as good as the people in your downline and never any better.

I once knew a distributor who allowed her downline in the basement of her house but refused to let them upstairs. She never understood that it was these very people who made it possible for her to live in a fine house. She never got it, and it eventually caught up with her.

Accept the fact that sooner or later a troublemaker or two will pop up like a weed in your organization. They're as easy to spot as crabgrass in your front yard. With any luck, you can teach these people not to gossip and fight with others in your downline. If not, continue to be pleasant to them, knowing that they will eventually fall to the wayside.

Master networkers are master peacekeepers with thick skin. They understand that the more successful they become, the more the negative types will want to throw spears into their back. They know that nothing is more vicious than a tongue out of control. Yet, they never fall into the trap of saying bad things about other people, not even the ones they don't like.

In *Tender Warriors* by Stu Weber, Sylvia Williams tells the story about how her husband, Pastor Orville Williams handled hateful calls. ''...Those sharp, venomous, critical calls that come at night when you're tired and emotionally low and have poured yourself out doing your best. As the calls would get longer and longer, Orville's voice would get softer and sweeter. That's how I knew the call was hurting him.''

It's important for networkers to like everyone. Heck, it doesn't take any skill to like someone you like. Anyone can do that. The master networker learns to like people they don't like. They have the unique ability to see only the good in people, and to teach others to do the same. The ones who learn this lesson are destined for greatness in the industry and in life.

I don't know if you have ever thought about it, but it is impossible to dislike someone that really likes you. When someone is constantly building you up, and telling you how terrific you are, you can't help liking them. It would be crazy not to. That's the same way that you want to treat everybody in your organization.

If you're a brand new distributor or a star, my advice to you is to stay out of the company politics. You're an independent contractor and your job is to build a distribution network. The company's job is to provide you with quality products and to send your checks out on time. It's really a very simple relationship that works like a charm if you let the company do its job and you do yours.

Don't start second guessing the president, the marketing department or the VP of sales. They're human, they'll make mistakes, but if you're in a good company, they'll do a lot more right things than they will wrong. But if you start complaining about them, guess what? Your downline will start complaining and second guessing the company, too.

The next thing you know they've quit because they stopped believing in the company that you sold them on. Your whining and complaining unsold them, and all because you thought you should have been in the new opportunity tape, or you didn't like the packaging of the new product, or because you think the president hired the wrong person in the marketing department, or that one of the scientists put too much vitamin C in the herbal tea. Hey, if this is the kind of stuff that excites you, you need to turn in your distributorship and get a job in corporate America. That's the very stuff that most networkers want to stay away from.

It's important for you to be a staunch supporter of your company and all the people in it. That's not to say that you won't have disagreements, because you will. If you have an idea, share it. If the company likes it, great. If they don't like it, don't go running around telling everyone in your organization how stupid the company is. Once a decision is made, support it as if was your idea. That's what good leaders and followers do.

I don't want to give you the impression that I've mastered all of these areas. The truth is that I'm still learning and trying hard to become a better person, a better distributor and a better leader in my organization. I know that I have a long way to go.

However, I will say that after spending some years in this industry that I have learned a lot about people. There is no occupation I know of that demands so much personal growth. If you'll learn to criticize others less and work on improving yourself more, you'll no doubt become a master networker.

Furthermore, as you learn to be a better person in your working life, you'll find that it will carry over into your personal life. If it makes sense to push up your distributors, then it makes sense to push up your spouse and your children. If you learn to put other people first in your business life, it only stands to reason to put your family first in your personal life. If criticism doesn't work on your downline, then it probably isn't doing much for your children or your spouse either.

Personal growth is one of the greatest rewards that MLM has to offer. When working with people, always keep in mind that you are not always working with people of logic, but people of emotion. If you run across someone who you really like, copy them, and if you run across someone who you can't stand, look at yourself.

In *The Chataine's Guardian,* Robin Hardy describes what she thinks is the ideal man. ''It is good for a man to be strong. A strong man can do many things. But a man who is both strong and gentle is wonderful. A man must be intelligent, of course, but if he is also humble, that makes him all the more appealing...a man who is strong enough to live a disciplined life, but who is tender with the faults of others...a man who is honest above all, but kind...a man with courage to stay with the same task year in and year out, even if it is boring or tiring or painful, simply because it is his duty...a man with the courage of faithfulness. I love all these things about a man.''

What Hardy says about an ideal man could, of course, be applied to an ideal woman.

Chapter 24

Don't Make Your People Weak

"There is no use whatever trying to help people who do not help themselves. You cannot push anyone up a ladder unless he is willing to climb himself."   — Andrew Carnegie

I f your goal is to create a large organization, it is essential that you make your people strong and independent from the start. Let them know that network marketing is a simple business that anyone can do. On the other hand, if you make it complicated, and your distributors feel as if they can't do it without you, you're going to be doing a lot of baby-sitting.

Granted, it always feels good to be needed. When a distributor says that you give the greatest presentations in the world and that they could never be as good as you, a red flag should go up immediately. Your job is not to make yourself the issue or to do presentations for all your people. If that were the case, your organization could only grow so big. Your job is to teach people what you do, so that they can do it and teach others to do the same.

It's a lot like being a mom or dad. As a parent, I love giving my children baths, brushing their hair and tying their shoes. It feels so good to be needed. The problem is that my job as a dad is to teach my children how to bathe themselves, brush their own hair and tie their own shoes. Not only that, but when they do these things on their own, it gives them a feeling of self-worth and confidence.

When Larry Garner and I were working together in Kennesaw, Georgia, we had a terrific time doing appointments and training new people. We worked right out of Larry's house, so in between appointments, I had time to spend with his children and his lovely wife, Linda. But after about 90 days, Larry was better at telling the Reliv story than I was.

"You know, Tom, you really don't need to come by tomorrow," he told me one afternoon. "I can do this thing on my own."

I got this hurt look on my face as I asked in a quiet voice, "Are you sure, Larry?"

"I'm sure," he answered.

Slowly, I turned and walked out the front door. As soon as I got outside, I threw my hands into the air, shouted "yes" and did a little victory dance. Larry was a mature distributor now, ready to tackle the world on his own. That meant I was free to go out and find someone else and duplicate myself again.

That didn't mean that Larry and I would never work together again, because we would, many times. What it meant was that he was ready to handle the lion's share of his business without my help. When he did need me, he would call, but the longer he was in the business, the less he leaned on me.

Through the years, I've watched plenty of networkers have a tough time letting a distributor go. They enjoy having their down-line depend on them and want to be involved in all aspects of their business. That may work in the beginning when your organization is small, but if you continue to build it that way, the day will come when your phone will never quit ringing, and you'll never have a moment to yourself.

Network marketing is not difficult. Anyone can do it. But if you're not careful, some people will take advantage of your time, and if enough people do that, it won't be long before you have no life. That's one of the reasons that I like business and training meetings.

Instead of spending countless hours each day and night running here and there, my distributors can bring their prospects to one place, and together we can talk to them at one time. Believe me, it's much easier to present the opportunity to 40 people at one time than it is to meet with 40 individuals at 40 different locations.

The biggest reason that I got into MLM was to have a life, to have time to spend with Karen and the children. If I didn't have great frontlines under me who ran their own organizations and taught their people to do the same, I would have to spend so much time on the phone and meeting with people that I would be worse off than I was before.

Today, I can take a month off or even a year. I am free to go to Maui or anywhere in the world with my family. Not only that, but when I get home, my check will be there and it will probably be bigger than the month before because the thousands of people in my organization don't need me to hold their hands while they work.

My greatest thrill in the business is to sit in the very back of a room and watch people in my downline honored on stage. I love to listen to them speak and train, and I chuckle to myself as I hear them use some of my words, stories, and wouldn't you know it, even my jokes. Now, that's duplication.

When Reliv came out with a new opportunity tape, I can't tell you how much I enjoyed watching Mindy Jones in it along with her daughter, Sarah. If Oscars were given for MLM opportunity tapes, Rick Moore certainly would have received one for sincerity. He was awesome, as was Michele Hembree and John Quirk. I remember these people when they were afraid to talk, now they're stars of screen and stage. Only in MLM.

Not long ago, a fellow asked me if all the money that I now make has changed me from the simple guy that once lived in a tiny starter home and drove a beat-up old van.

Looking him square in the eyes, I said, "No, way. I still enjoy the simple things in life...like listening to the pitter-patter of rain...bounce off the top of my Mercedes."

But there would be no Mercedes if I didn't understand the importance of duplication and making my people strong.

Chapter 25

Fun And Unfun

"He has achieved success who has lived well, laughed often, and loved much." — Bessie Anderson Stanley

L ife can be divided into two distinct categories — fun and unfun. When we were children, we chased after fun with huge smiles plastered across our freckled faces. As a boy, all that my older sisters had to do to get me excited was to suggest a game of tag or hide-and-go-seek. You could count me in when the kids in the neighborhood were looking for player for a game of sandlot baseball. This was fun stuff, and I loved every minute of it.

On the other hand, I was quick to skedaddle when my dad announced that he was looking for volunteers to weed the front hedge or clean the garage. Doing the dishes after supper, especially when you consider that there were seven children in my family, was definitely unfun. No doubt about it, nothing is more difficult than finding a kid around when there are chores to be done.

Now, I ask you, do you think we're any different today just because we're taller and have to shave or choose to wear high heels? I don't think so. Most of us are like little otters who love to play and have a good time. It's like the bumper sticker that reads: *"A bad day on the golf course is better than a good day at work."*

Getting a couple of buddies together to go trout fishing is a whole lot easier than getting them to come over and help you clean the basement. If Karen is having a bad day, all I have to do to put a smile on her face is say, "Hey, honey, let's go to the mall and see if we can find you a dazzling new outfit." Shopping is unfun for me, but it sure is fun for her.

One of the problems with life is that it is so full of unfun. So often bosses make the workplace miserable. Many teachers make learning in the classroom a bore, and parents, caught up in the toil of day-to-day survival, often take themselves so seriously that they take the fun out of the home.

A few years ago, I went to Dresden, Ohio, where I toured a company called Longaberger Baskets. Each year, hundreds of millions of dollars worth of baskets are sold by Longaberger's direct sales force. The company's founder, Dave Longaberger, believes in the power of fun so much that inside the lobby of his main building there is a sign that reads, *"Each work day should be at least 20 percent fun."*

The bottom line is simple: if you're having fun, people will follow you, because people like to do fun things. That's why it's so important for you to have fun while you're building your organization. If you're not, you're doing something wrong.

Some of the best times that I've ever had in my life were at Reliv parties. I'm a big believer in getting together with distributors on a frequent basis. It allows them to get to know one another, and to learn from one another in a relaxed atmosphere. We've even had parties where distributors brought guests. We didn't pitch them on the business or the products; we simply showed them how much fun we had together.

In Atlanta, Mindy Jones had the best house for entertaining and in the two years that Karen and I lived in Georgia, I don't think a month went by without a party there. All the distributors brought their favorite casseroles or desserts, and we'd sit around and eat and tell stories. It was there that many of us became friends and made a commitment to work hard and have fun with one another for the rest of our lives.

Fun is certainly part of the Reliv culture. To this end, the company has taken its top people on trips to Maui, the Greek islands,

Cancun, Australia and other exciting places around the world. People want to have fun, and it's amazing how hard they will work in order to experience an adventure with friends.

You can bet when we're on these vacations that Rod Devereux, Rick Moore and I will be challenging Tom Moody, Shawn Bergeron and Mike Darraugh to a golf match. We're not all in the same lines, but we sure have become close friends. We've also played most of the great courses in the world together.

Rod Devereux telephoned me recently to ask if I would be willing to come out to California for a few days and work with some of his people. Rod's not only a master networker, he's a master arm-twister.

"It's 80 degrees in Southern California and the golf courses are in perfect condition," he said. "We can do a little work and play a little golf. What do you say?"

Considering that it was snowing in Missouri at the time, my answer was simple: "Yes, and how many strokes are you going to give me?"

One summer, Karen and I spent a glorious few weeks in Australia and New Zealand. During that time, we frittered away one delightful day and night sailing in Sydney on a beautiful yacht owned by Brian Folbigg, the same chap I had met in Mindy's living room a couple of years earlier. We sat on the deck and gazed at the clear blue water as the sparkling lights of Sydney glowed in the distance.

As we munched on caviar-covered crackers and nibbled at giant shrimp, Karen and I would glance at each other and say, "Can you believe we're really doing this?"

During a cruise to the Bahamas, Don Gibbons, Reliv's vice president of United States Sales, led the way in a bevy of beach games on a deserted island on the tropical part of the Atlantic.

"This is what it's all about," Don said just after we were eliminated from the water-balloon-toss contest. "We're going to travel the world together with our best friends and have fun. Isn't it great, Tom?"

"It would be even better," I replied, "if you'd learn how to toss a water balloon."

Chapter 26

Be Sure To Set Goals

"Become a possibilitarian. No matter how dark things seem to be or actually are, raise your sights and see possibilities — always see them, for they're always there."
— Norman Vincent Peale

I 've always been a big believer in goal-setting. There's no doubt that there is great power in the mind if you feed it properly and give it direction. The problem is most of us seldom take the time to empower our subconscious.

Not setting goals for yourself as you start your MLM career makes about as much sense as taking off on a vacation without knowing where you're going. Tragically, most of us go through life that way. We're like ships sailing out to sea without a rudder to steer us, or a compass to guide us. Is it any wonder that many of us don't get anywhere in life — we don't even know where we're supposed to be heading.

In my mind, the difference between a goal and a dream is that a goal is written down. And when you write your goals down, make sure that you are specific about them. For example, it's not enough to say that you want to make lots of money. The truth is, it's not the money that you want, but what you think that money can bring you.

The first goal that I wrote down was to make enough money so that Karen could stay home with the children. There was nothing in the world that she wanted more than to be at home with her three kids. You'll find that oftentimes you'll work harder to help others achieve their goals than you will your own.

The day that Karen became a full-time mom was not only one of the happiest days of my life, but also a glorious day for Karen and the children. In my book and accompanying audio tape, *The Male Homemaker's Handbook or Never Kiss a Kid Who's Just Eaten a Toad,* I wrote: "My heart was doing cartwheels. As I regarded my family and saw their happiness, I knew that this was the day that no kids would cry...Mom was going to be home and so was I, and all because of that little business that I had started working off our kitchen table."

The funny thing about that scene is that I had witnessed it in my mind a hundred times. I dreamed it, I felt it, and I even knew when it was going to happen. And it did.

Another goal that I had was to get a proper home for my family, one that had a bedroom for each of the children and a backyard where they could play. It wasn't enough to just think about it, I wrote it down. Not only that, but I had Karen cut a picture out of a magazine of a house that she dreamed of and I taped it to the bathroom mirror. That way, I could see it each morning as I prepared to start my day.

Next to the picture of what Karen called a "proper house," I wrote in red lipstick the number 5. I knew in my mind that if I would just go out every day and talk to five new people about my great products and opportunity that within a year we would live in that house. I never put my head on my pillow unless I had done that, and I never went to sleep without thinking about it.

Within a year, Karen and I bought a house that looked almost identical to the one on our mirror. The house was near Atlanta, a community where we dreamed of living, and the backyard was so big that we had a half-acre vegetable garden, something that we always wanted. Near the garden was a play area for the children, equipped with swings, slides, monkey bars, play houses and a giant sandbox.

I think it's critical that you set down a series of short- and long-term goals. Don't be afraid to dream big. Aim for the stars.

Let's say your first goal is to buy a new car. Again, you need to be specific, so head down to the nearest car lot and find the one that you want. Sit in it, test drive it, and get a picture of it and stick it on your refrigerator or in your office.

Now, come up with a simple plan of action to get your dream car. Maybe it involves talking to five people daily, or handing out 100 flyers, or passing out five opportunity tapes, or taking one new person a week to the business meeting. The key is to come up with a plan and then work that plan.

Keep in mind, too, that it's not good enough to talk to five people one day and then not talk to anyone for a week. You must be consistent with your efforts. You might find it helpful to share your goal with someone in your upline who you can hold you accountable.

One of the most common goals that new networkers have is to leave their job and do MLM full-time. Certainly it is a worthy goal, but one that you must handle carefully. I've always told new distributors that to do that they must first replace their current income. Too many times, I've watched people jump in full-time before they were ready.

To do that you must be a real self-starter and a real workhorse. Most people aren't. I think Andrew Carnegie put it best when he said, ''The average person puts only 25 percent of his energy and ability into his work. The world takes off its hat to those who put in more than 50 percent of their capacity, and stands on its head for those few and far between souls who devote 100 percent.''

One of the goals that I wrote down early in my career was to buy my mom and dad a new car. With seven kids to support, they usually drove clunkers, and I was determined that one day I would show my appreciation for all that they had given me. A new car seemed like just the ticket. The problem was that most of my adult life I couldn't afford to get myself a new car let alone one for my folks.

But Reliv changed all of that. Now, I could dream again, and I started asking Dad what kind of car he would really like to have. I worked even harder when I learned that Mom's old bomb had broken down one night, leaving her stranded in the middle of nowhere.

There is no higher goal in my mind than trying to help others. And so it was, on my mom and dad's 50th wedding anniversary, Karen and I gave my folks a brand new car. It was one of the happiest days of my life, and I can tell you that I received more joy from that gift than they did.

If you haven't done it already, take the time to write down short-term, long-term and life-long goals. Then review them each morning and talk about them to the important people in your life. Keep in mind, too, that your goals will probably change as you go along, so don't be afraid to revise them.

Some of the best times that Karen and I have today is sitting around and talking about what we want to do and accomplish with our lives. Sometimes, it's fun stuff like where we want to take the children for vacation, and sometimes it's serious stuff like what do we need to do to make our marriage better. We recently watched a series of video tapes by Gary Smalley designed to strengthen loving relationships.

In the series, Smalley asked the wives to rate their marriages on a one-to-10 basis, 10 being the best. I was pretty confident that Karen would give us an eight or nine. You can imagine my shock when she said it was "about a six, maybe a seven."

Then Smalley asked where we wanted it to be. Naturally, Karen told me she wanted it to be a 10. That was her goal and mine, too.

The next step was to write down the things that we needed to work on in order to get it to a 10. Karen quickly put together a hefty list.

"Listen, honey," I said. "Do you think that you could start by giving me your Top 10. I'm not sure I can work on all that stuff at one time."

The point is this: we have a goal of getting to 10, and we have a plan, a map if you will, to follow in order to get there. By the way, I'm now up to an eight, which I'm pretty excited about.

You could do the same thing with your business. On a one to 10, where would you place your networking business right now, and on a one-to-10 basis, and where do you want it to be? Now, in order to get it there, what are the things that you must do on a daily bases?

Not long ago, my dad and I were sitting out on the deck of my new home outside of St. Louis.

"Did you ever dream that you would live in a home like this?" my dad asked. "It's incredible."

"You bet I did," I answered without hesitating for a second. "I dreamed about it constantly. That's why it happened."

Now that you have taken the time to set down some goals, go after them. Do it. Make it happen. And never, never, never, give up. Simply aim for the highest, and you'll be surprised at what glorious things can happen to your life.

Chapter 27

Someone Pinch Me Because I Must Be Dreaming

"The end of labor is to gain leisure."   — Aristotle

Each morning, when I wake up, I ask Karen to give me a great big pinch, because I feel like I must be dreaming. It's hard to believe that in 1989, we lived in that tiny home in Florida, and both of us worked all the time in an unsuccessful effort to pay our bills. In those days, we had little time for the children. Now, I help coach Tommy's baseball team and have ample time to chauffeur Lindsay and Ashley to their dance and music classes.

During a weekday last year, when most fathers were busy working, I watched from my coaching position at first base as Tommy came to bat in the last inning with his team trailing by two runs with two outs and two runners on. My stomach tightened as he quickly took two strikes. Then it happened.

On the next pitch, my little buddy smashed a towering home run over the centerfield fence to win the game. I was shocked. Never before had I seen a Little Leaguer smack one out of that park. As Tommy half-ran and half-jumped his way toward first base, I knew that I had just experienced one of the great moments in his life and mine.

"I'm so happy I could cry," he said to me as he rounded the bag.

I was already crying. I knew, too, that if I had a regular job, I probably never would have shared that moment. I sent up a little prayer of thanks as my little slugger rounded the bases and jumped on home, where he was swarmed by his cheering teammates.

The smash was the result of us spending a lot of time together working on his hitting. I threw pitches to him by the hours and, in winter, we went to the indoor batting cages. Reliv had given me the time to spend with my son. It could offer no greater reward.

Today, we live in a spectacular home atop a hill that looks down on two of the most magnificent golf courses in the state of Missouri. From my home office, I can look out across a valley that is nestled in between rolling hills and creeks. The kids and I spend our summers exploring the banks of the nearby Missouri River and looking for Indian arrowheads in the same fields that Lewis and Clark once camped.

When the children are in school, Karen and I work out together, go antiquing, play golf, help out at our church, take long walks and fall more and more in love. When the children are at home, we bike down to the country club, where we play golf and tennis and swim by the hours. When we're not enjoying our new home and community, we take long vacations to all sorts of exotic places.

Not long ago, I was playing golf with David Kreher, Reliv's chief operations officer and a good friend. As we came to the 17th tee behind my house, he looked up and said, "When you have a home like that with a golf course in your backyard, it sure must be hard to leave."

"It is," I said.

Today, when prospects come to my home, they immediately know that it is possible to do big things in MLM. One of the ironies of the industry is that the more success you have in the business, the easier the business is to do. Although I don't have to drive myself anymore, I am still active and am proud to attend weekly meetings and training's held in St. Louis.

I like being around networkers, I guess. Oftentimes, local distributors bring folks out to my house. I don't mind. I love telling people about the incredible opportunity that awaits those who aren't afraid to work and dare to believe in themselves. A lot of times, I play golf with the prospects. Heck, it's just as easy to network on a golf course as it is in an office. Besides, it's fun, and you know how I feel about fun.

A while back I rounded up the family and went to Florida, where we spent four days at the Magic Kingdom. I've never seen children have so much fun from morning to night. Taking the kids to Disney World and doing it up right was one of the goals on my list.

On our first morning, we had breakfast with the Disney characters and Tommy sat right next to Goofy and told him how much he liked his cartoons.

Tommy was so excited about eating breakfast with Goofy that he talked about it for the rest of the day.

Karen's outlook on the matter was a bit different. "I don't know what the big deal was," she said to me with a grin and a wink. "I've been eating breakfast with goofy for years."

Later that day, as we walked down main street and saw Cinderella's castle in the distance, I looked over at Karen and saw tears rolling down her cheeks.

"What's wrong, honey?" I asked. "Are you all right?"

"I'm perfect," she said. "I was just thinking about the time that we were going to bring the kids here and we couldn't because you wrecked your van."

"That seems like a million years ago," I said. "That was such a terrible day. I felt like such a loser."

Karen pulled me to the side and looked straight in to my eyes. "Darling, you were never a loser," she said. "You just needed to find something that you could put your heart into. Something that you believed in."

She drew me close to her and gave me a big kiss right there in front of Mickey Mouse and his friends. I didn't mind, and when Ashley saw us kissing, she quickly ran over and hugged our legs.

"I'm so proud of you," Karen whispered in my ear. "I never quit believing in you."

Now, I was beginning to tear up. I turned away to wipe my eyes with my shirtsleeve, and when I did, I saw the reflection of my family in a store window. Tommy, wearing his new Goofy hat, long ears and all, Lindsay and Ashley giggling and laughing, and Karen and I holding hands. We looked like the all-American family in the all-American place. Who says the American dream is dead? We're proof that it's alive, and it's called multi-level marketing.